Copyright Page

MW01602127

Late Night With the Word: Genesis Season 1
© 2025 by Shavone Williams
All rights reserved.

No part of this book may be reproduced, stored in a retrieval system, or transmitted in any form or by any means—electronic, mechanical, photocopying, recording, or otherwise—without the prior written permission of the publisher, except for brief quotations used in reviews or articles.

Scripture quotations are taken from the *King James Version* (KJV) of the Holy Bible.
Public Domain.

This book is a work of creative biblical reflection. While based on Scripture, the interview format and dialogues are literary interpretations intended to help readers engage the Word of God in a fresh, inspired way.

Printed in the United States of America
First Edition | ISBN 979-8-218-84797-5

Published by Oracle Publishing Group

About the Author

Shavone Williams was born and raised in Freeport, Grand Bahama, Bahamas, where she grew up in a strong Christian home as the youngest of three children and the only girl. Her early foundation in faith shaped her lifelong passion for God's Word and her desire to teach it with clarity, creativity, and conviction.

She holds a Master's Degree in Christian Education and an undergraduate degree in Pre-Law/Criminal Justice. Shavone currently serves as a Minister in Training (MIT) at New Generation Church in New York, where she continues to grow in ministry and leadership.

For more than five years, she has faithfully led an online teaching ministry called Kingdom Mindset for Kingdom Living, where she empowers believers to study the Word of God and apply Kingdom principles to everyday life.

Late Night With the Word is her first book, a heartfelt and Spirit-led creation that brings biblical truth to life in a talk show–inspired format. Shavone's mission is to help people see that God's Word is not distant or outdated, but alive, relatable, and full of power for today.

Dedication

This book is lovingly dedicated to my father,

Truman Napoleon Williams

July 16, 1952 – March 30, 2023

"Forever in my heart."

Your strength, your work ethic, and the life lessons you taught me helped shape who I am today.

You showed me what it means to be resilient, to keep going, and to find my own way.

Your influence left a lasting mark on my journey, and I will always honor the part you played in helping me become the woman God called me to be.

Fun Fact About This Season

I wrote most of *Late Night With the Word: Genesis* while sitting on the floor.
That became my creative space whenever inspiration struck.

Honestly, I typed in the oddest places. I didn't limit myself to a desk — I followed the Holy Spirit. Wherever He dropped the idea, that's where I opened my laptop.

Most of my inspiration flowed after 1 p.m. I don't know what it is about that hour, but something heavenly tends to happen after lunch.

Also, I interviewed anything and anyone. If it moved — or didn't — it probably got a mic.

And just when I thought I was finished, I added thirteen more episodes and four bonus ones. Because when God is still speaking, you don't shut the laptop.

II

Introduction

Late Night With the Word: Genesis (Season 1)

Welcome to *Late Night With the Word: Genesis, Season 1* — a devotional experience like no other.

This book was born out of something deeply personal: a lifelong dream and a God-given calling.
Since I was twenty-one years old, I've dreamed of being a talk show host. I imagined sitting on a stage, asking deep and meaningful questions, connecting with guests in ways that make people feel seen, heard, and inspired. But I never expected God would take that dream and merge it with the deepest passion of my heart — teaching His Word.

Now, at thirty-eight, after years of studying, praying, and sharing the gospel, the Holy Spirit has turned that dream into purpose. *Late Night With the Word* is more than a clever format — it's a ministry. It's how God has called me to teach: through creativity, conversation, and connection.

This book is a **talk show–inspired devotional**, where the Word of God takes center stage and biblical characters take the hot seat. It's fun, fresh, and full of life — but most of all, it's rooted in Scripture and reverence for God.

My passion for this book didn't come from trying to do something trendy. It came from a desire to make the Bible **accessible, engaging, and unforgettable.** I love the Word. I love teaching it. And I love helping people discover its truth for themselves.

That's why each chapter in this book is styled like an episode — complete with a host monologue, a character interview, a "The Big Truth" moment, and a closing prayer. My hope is that as you read, it won't just feel like you're reading a devotional — it'll feel like you're sitting right there in the studio, listening in on heaven's conversations.

This book is for those who are hungry to understand the Bible but have struggled to connect with it in the past. It's for people who need something *different* to spark their faith. It's for those who love creative storytelling but crave biblical truth. It's for the Bible teacher, the podcast lover, the late-night thinker, and the early-morning worshipper.

It's for people like me.
And for people like you.

"All scripture is given by inspiration of God, and is profitable for doctrine, for reproof, for correction, for instruction in righteousness."
— *2 Timothy 3:16 (KJV)*

Genesis was the perfect place to start because it's where everything began. But more importantly, it's where we first see the heart of God — His creativity, His holiness, His justice, His mercy, and His relentless commitment to redeem mankind. Every verse carries weight. Every story carries truth. And through this book, I hope to bring those truths to life in a way that draws you into deeper relationship with Jesus Christ.

"Thy word is a lamp unto my feet, and a light unto my path."

— Psalm 119:105 (KJV)

As a teacher of the Word, I believe the Bible is not just meant to be studied — it's meant to be **experienced**. It's alive. It speaks. It convicts, comforts, challenges, and transforms.

That's why I wrote this book — not just to share Bible stories, but to create encounters. I want you to see how every chapter of Genesis speaks to your own story, your own struggles, and your own calling. Whether you're wrestling like Jacob, waiting like Sarah, or dreaming like Joseph, there is something here for you.

This book isn't about me — it's about what God can do when we say *yes* to Him.
It's about the **collision of calling and creativity.**
It's about the late nights when God speaks and we finally slow down enough to hear Him.
It's about using every gift He's given us for His glory.

So if you've ever wanted to fall in love with Scripture…
If you've ever longed for a creative way to connect with the Word…
If you've ever felt called to teach or share but didn't know where to start…
This is for you.

And this is only the beginning.

Late Night with the Word: Genesis Season 1

Let the show begin.

Shavonne Williams, Host & Author

SEASON PREVIEWS

SEASON PREVIEWS (CONT.)

SEASON PREVIEWS (CONT.)

Episode 1: God – The Original Creator

Theme: *Before there was a who, there was a Him*
Scripture: *Genesis 1:1 (KJV)* — "In the beginning God created the heaven and the earth."

Opening Monologue

Have you ever walked into a room before anyone else?
No furniture. No food. Just awkward stillness in the air and silence.

Now imagine walking into that kind of room — except the room doesn't even exist yet. That's how God entered *Genesis.*

He didn't just show up early; He showed up before time began. No welcome party. No audience. No likes.
Just God — and the void.

But here's what's wild: when He spoke, the void listened.

Before there were prophets, priests, or praise teams, there was God.
He didn't need a choir to feel worthy.
He didn't wait on feedback to move forward.
He simply opened His mouth and said, *"Let there be light."*
And the universe had no choice but to obey.

So tonight, we start our show with the One who doesn't just show up — He starts the show.

Guest of the Night: God – The Original Creator

Ladies and gentlemen, our first guest is the reason you even have breath to hear this.

He's the Author and the Finisher, the Alpha and the Omega, the Star-Breather, and the Life-Giver.

Give it up for **GOD!**

Host:

God, welcome. It's beyond an honor to have You on.

God:

I Am.

Host:

(Laughs) Okay! Starting strong. So take us back to *Genesis 1* — what moved You to begin?

God:

I wanted relationship. I created out of love, out of desire, out of purpose.

Everything I made was intentional. There was no mistake in My creation.

Host:

And when You said, *"Let there be light,"* was that metaphorical? Literal? How does that work?

God:

When I speak, what doesn't exist has no choice but to exist. My Word is life.

Host:

For those listening who feel like their life is dark, empty, or chaotic — what would You say to them?

God:

I'm not afraid of darkness. I don't need perfect conditions to create.

I do My best work in emptiness.

I spoke into the void then, and I'm still speaking into it now.

The Big Truth

Genesis 1:1 says:

"In the beginning God created the heaven and the earth."

Everything in your life flows from your starting point.
And *Genesis* makes it clear: **God is the start.**
Not your pain. Not your plans. Not your past. Just God.

You don't build a house starting with the furniture — you start with the foundation.
God is the foundation of all things.
If He's not first, nothing else will stand.

God is the Origin, not the Option.
We often treat God like a backup plan when things go wrong,
but *Genesis* makes it clear He was first.
If we put Him first, everything else aligns.

God creates out of chaos.
The earth was without form and void — formless, empty, dark.
And yet He spoke light, order, beauty, and purpose into it.
What God did for the earth, He can do for you.

God finishes what He starts.
When God said, *"It is good,"* it wasn't just a compliment — it was a conclusion.
He rested not because He was tired, but because the work

was complete.
And the same God who finishes worlds will finish what He started in you.

You were made on purpose, for purpose.
Later in *Genesis 1* we find that God made man in His image.
That means you're not random.
You are not your failures.
You are not what the void tried to tell you.
You carry the breath of the Creator.

Closing Prayer

I declare that God is the Author of my beginning.
I was not created by accident — I am part of a divine design.
Darkness will not stop the light God is speaking over me.
The same God who created the heavens and the earth is working on my behalf.
And because He's in my beginning, I know He's already written my ending.

End of Episode 1

Next time on Late Night with the Word...
We sit down with the man who dropped the ball but couldn't hide from grace.
That's right — **Adam is in the building.**

4

Episode 2: Host & Adam

Theme: *God formed him with care, then brought him someone who completed the scene.*

Scripture:

Genesis 2:7 — "And the Lord God formed man of the dust of the ground."

Genesis 2:22 — "And brought her unto the man."

Opening Monologue

Tonight's guest needs no introduction — but we're giving him one anyway.
He was the first man, the first worshipper, the first gardener, and yes — unfortunately — the first to fumble the bag.

But before all of that, he had a moment no one else in human history can claim:
He was created by the hands of God — not spoken into being like the stars or the sea, but *formed.*

Then he woke up in paradise, saw animals, trees, rivers, and sky — but none of it compared to the moment God brought him *her.*

Tonight, we talk formation, naming animals, and that first look at the woman who stole his rib and his heart.
Please give it up for our brother from the beginning…
Adam!

Interview: Host × Adam

Host:
Adam, welcome! First human in history — it's a pleasure.

Adam:
Glad to be here. Never done a talk show, but I've had a lot of alone time to think about things.

Host:
Let's start at the beginning — literally. What's your first memory?

Adam:
Dust. Then… breath. Imagine waking up, and your first breath is the actual Spirit of God.
I didn't just feel alive — I felt *known*. His hands shaped me.
I wasn't just made — I was molded.

Host:
You weren't *called* into existence…

Adam:
No, I was *sculpted*. God got low — into the dirt — and formed me. That alone says something about how personal I am to Him.
Then He gave me purpose right away. Told me to tend the garden, name animals, and walk in dominion. Everything had structure.

Host:
But even in paradise, something was missing.

Adam:
Yeah. I had beauty, peace, work — but no one to share it with.

8

God said, *"It's not good for man to be alone."*
And I think He said that not because I was complaining, but because He already knew I was made for relationship.

Host:
And then she enters.

Adam:
Whew… Listen. I was knocked out — deep sleep, next-level rest. When I woke up, I saw her walking toward me, and I promise, the air changed.

Host:
What did you feel in that moment?

Adam:
It wasn't just attraction — it was *recognition.* I saw me — but more beautiful, more graceful.
She didn't come from the dust. She came from my side.
That's why I said, *"This is now bone of my bones and flesh of my flesh."*

Host:
You didn't just meet her — you met *you* in her.

Adam:
Exactly. She was the rhythm to my breath. God didn't just give me a helper — He gave me a reflection of His image in another form.

Host:
That's powerful. So you were formed by God's hands, breathed into by His Spirit, placed with purpose, and given love…

9

Adam:

…and I still messed it up.

Host:

But God didn't leave you there.

Adam:

No, He didn't. He came looking for us — even after we sinned.

That's the heart of God. Judgment came, yes — but so did mercy.

He covered us with skins. He didn't let us leave the garden naked.

The Big Truth

1. You Weren't Spoken into Being — You Were Shaped

Genesis 2:7 — "And the Lord God formed man of the dust of the ground."

This tells us your identity isn't casual — it's intentional.

You weren't just made to exist; you were made to reflect the One who made you.

When God formed Adam:

He didn't outsource the job.

He didn't skip steps.

He didn't use a template.

He formed him — then breathed into him.

You weren't made for mass production. You were made for divine purpose.

2. God Places You Before He Pairs You

Genesis 2:15 — "And the Lord God took the man, and put him into the garden."

Adam didn't get a woman first — he got *placed* first.
He had a location, a calling, and responsibility.

Many people want their Eve (or Adam) before they've been planted in purpose.
God's order is this:
Formation → Placement → Purpose → Partnership.

He didn't bring Eve while Adam was lost; He brought her when Adam was walking in obedience.

3. God Doesn't Give You What You Want — He Gives You What You're Ready For

Genesis 2:18 — "It is not good that the man should be alone."

Notice: Adam never said he was lonely — God observed it.
And in His perfect timing, He made provision.

God didn't just give Adam anyone — He gave him a woman crafted from his own rib.
That's proximity to the heart. That's protection. That's unity.

God doesn't rush relationships. He reveals them when we're ready to handle them.

11

4. Love Starts with Recognition, Not Just Attraction

Genesis 2:23 — "This is now bone of my bones and flesh of my flesh."

Adam didn't flirt. He didn't fumble. He didn't waste time. The moment he saw Eve, he recognized her.

Godly connection comes with *clarity,* not confusion. When it's from God, you won't just see a body — you'll see purpose.

5. God Still Covers Us After We Fall

Even after Adam and Eve sinned, God didn't walk away in disgust — He walked toward them in compassion.

Genesis 3:21 — "Unto Adam also and to his wife did the Lord God make coats of skins, and clothed them."

That's grace.
The same hands that formed Adam in the beginning still covered him after the fall.

Let this truth sit deep:
You may mess up. You may fall.
But the hands that made you will never abandon you.

Prayer

Father,
Thank You for forming me with Your hands and breathing life into me with Your Spirit.
I am not an accident. I am not random. I was shaped by You — on purpose, for purpose.

Help me to trust Your timing and Your order.
Teach me to wait for placement before partnership.
Teach me to recognize what You send, instead of chasing what You never meant for me.

Just like You brought Eve to Adam, I believe You will bring the right things into my life when I am walking in obedience and purpose.

God, even in the places where I've fallen, thank You for being the One who still comes looking for me.
You don't leave me in shame — You cover me in grace.
The same hands that formed me still hold me even now.

Let my heart stay open to Your voice.
Let my life reflect the image You placed inside me.
And let me always remember: You are the One who started this, and You are faithful to finish it.

In Jesus' name, Amen.

End of Episode 2

Up next on Late Night with the Word:
She was formed from a rib, walked into paradise, and faced a choice that echoed through eternity.
Eve takes the stage. You don't wanna miss it.

Episode 3: Host & Eve

Theme: *She was formed with care, walked into beauty, faced a choice, and still carried purpose.*

Scripture: *Genesis 2:22 (KJV)* — "And the rib, which the Lord God had taken from man, made He a woman, and brought her unto the man."

Opening Monologue

Tonight's guest is a legend — the first woman, the first wife, the first to walk into paradise like it was home.
And let's be honest: she had the kind of entrance every queen deserves.

No birth certificate. No baby photos.
Just *boom* — woman in full glory.

She's known as *the mother of all living,* but her name has been dragged through every sermon, meme, and midnight Bible study ever since she took a bite.

But let's pause the judgment and meet the woman for real.

Tonight, she talks about what it was like waking up in Eden, seeing Adam for the first time, learning from him, and being faced with a serpent, a fruit, and a life-altering decision.

Put your hands together for our special guest — **Eve!**

15

Interview: Host × Eve

Host:
Eve, welcome to the show. I've got to say — you look flawless.

Eve:
Thank you. It's the garden glow. And — well — I was handcrafted.

Host:
Let's take it back. What's your first memory?

Eve:
I woke up surrounded by beauty — trees swaying, rivers flowing, flowers I couldn't even name yet.
And then I turned and saw him.

Host:
Adam?

Eve:
Yes. I didn't know his name yet, but I felt drawn. Like I knew him.
And I did — because I came from him. My body remembered his rib.
It wasn't romance. It was *recognition.*

Host:
Whewww. So what happened next?

Eve:
God brought me to him. And Adam just… spoke.
He called me *woman.*
Then he told me about the garden — about our purpose, the trees, the beauty, the work.

16

He also told me about one thing in particular…

Host:
The tree?

Eve:
Yes. *That* one, he said — the tree of the knowledge of good and evil.
He told me what God said: *Don't eat it. Don't even touch it.*
Everything else was ours, but that tree belonged to God.

Host:
What did you think when you heard that?

Eve:
I trusted it — at first. There was no reason not to.
But then curiosity crept in. I kept walking past it.
I kept looking at it. I started wondering why it was so off-limits.

Host:
And then came the serpent.

Eve:
(Pauses) Yes. He was subtle — not aggressive, not scary — just smooth.
He questioned what I'd been told. He said, *"Did God really say that?"*
And I listened.

Host:
And you took the bite.

Eve:
Yes. And in one bite, I broke trust — not just with God, but with myself, with Adam, with creation.

Host:

What did it feel like after?

Eve:

Shame. I had never felt shame before.
I felt exposed. Vulnerable.
And for the first time, I felt distant from God.

Host:

But did God abandon you?

Eve:

No. He came looking for us.
He asked questions — not because He didn't know, but
because He still cared.
He clothed us. He covered us.
And even in consequence, He left a promise — that from my
seed would come redemption.

The Big Truth

Eve's story is one of beauty and brokenness — but it's also
one of hope.
She was the first to fall, yes — but also the first to carry
promise.

1. God Brings You Into What He Already Prepared

Eve didn't wake up in a mess — she woke up in order.
She didn't have to build the garden — she walked into it.
That's grace.

Genesis 2:22 — "And brought her unto the man."

Before Eve had a voice, she had a place.
And the same is true for you.

2. Instruction Always Comes Before Temptation

Eve wasn't clueless.
She received instruction before the enemy ever approached.
That's how the enemy works — he targets what God already said.

Genesis 3:1 — "Yea, hath God said…?"

That's why we have to guard God's Word in our hearts like treasure.

3. You Can Be in the Right Place but Still Make the Wrong Choice

The garden was perfect.
The atmosphere was divine.
The surroundings were peaceful.

But even in the right place, disobedience can still grow if we entertain the wrong voices.

4. Shame Tries to Hide You but God Always Comes Looking

Eve and Adam hid — and we still do the same.
We hide behind busyness, behind guilt, behind *"I'm fine."*

But God never hides from us.

Genesis 3:9 — "And the Lord God called unto Adam, and

said unto him, Where art thou?"

He didn't call to condemn — He called to cover.

5. God Uses the Same Womb That Fell to Birth Redemption

Eve was told that her seed — her line — would one day crush the serpent's head (*Genesis 3:15*).

The same woman who brought the fruit to Adam would also carry the bloodline of Jesus.
Only God can flip a fall into a future like that.

Prayer

Lord, Thank You for forming me with intention and bringing me into what You already prepared.
Like Eve, I was made with care. I was made with purpose. I was brought into a place of promise — and I thank You.

Forgive me for the times I've listened to voices that questioned what You said — for the moments when curiosity overpowered obedience, for when I reached for what wasn't mine and ended up feeling shame instead of satisfaction.

But even in that, You still came for me.
You didn't leave me naked in my mistake.
You clothed me with mercy.
You corrected me with love.
And You spoke hope into my future, even when I couldn't see it.

Help me to guard Your Word in my heart.

20

Help me to recognize the serpent's lies.
And help me remember that even when I fall, You never cancel my calling.

Thank You for turning my failure into a future — for using my story to birth something eternal.

In Jesus' name, Amen.

End of Episode 3

Next time on Late Night with the Word...
The garden was silent. The fruit had been bitten.
And something entered the world that had never been heard before — a final breath.

It didn't come from the serpent.
It didn't come from Eve.
It came from *justice*.

Up next, we sit down with the one who didn't knock — but still entered.
Death is in the studio.

And tonight, we ask the question…
Was it punishment, or was it purpose?

Bonus Episode: Death — The Spirit Justice Called In

Theme: *Sin doesn't just make mistakes — it invites consequences.*

Genesis 2:17 (KJV) — *"But of the tree of the knowledge of good and evil, thou shalt not eat of it: for in the day that thou eatest thereof thou shalt surely die."*

Opening Monologue

Let's set the record straight.
Satan didn't invent death.
God did.

Not as a weapon — but as a warning.

Before Adam and Eve ever fell, God made it clear:
if they crossed the line, death would be the consequence.
It wasn't a scare tactic.
It was a boundary with weight.

And when disobedience came, so did death.

Tonight, we speak with a spirit that doesn't just symbolize endings — it represents justice.
Not the devil's tool, but God's response.

Guest of the Night: Death

Host:
Tonight's guest is not darkness, not evil — but consequence.
Please welcome the one most try to avoid: **Death.**

Death:
I wasn't in the garden at first. I wasn't needed.

23

There was no disobedience — only glory.
But when the Word of the Lord was violated, I was summoned.

Host:
So you're saying you didn't come by choice?

Death:
No. I come by command.
I'm not chaos — I'm order.
A response. A boundary that was crossed.

Host:
Most people assume Satan brought you in.

Death:
Then they don't know the Word.
God Himself said, *"You shall surely die."*
I was created to enforce what holiness requires.
Satan tempted, but he couldn't summon me.
Only God's justice could.

Host:
What was your first assignment like — entering a world that had only known life?

Death:
It was heavy.
I came quietly — not with a sword, but with separation.
The light in man dimmed.
The connection with God cracked.
The ground began to rot.
Something eternal became temporary.

Host:
And from then on, you've been part of the story.

24

Death:
Yes. But I'm not the end of the story.
I'm a doorway.
For those in rebellion, I'm final.
But for those who walk with God, I'm a transition.

Host:
Do you fear the day you'll be destroyed?

Death:
I was never meant to be eternal.
The Lamb was slain before the foundation of the world.
I know my time is marked.
One day, I will be swallowed up by victory.

The Big Truth

Death is not the enemy of God — it's the **servant of justice.**
It came not because Satan had power, but because
disobedience broke covenant.

God warned us in love.
The promise of death wasn't cruelty — it was clarity.

Death is the wage of sin, but not the end of the story.
In Christ, death becomes a passage, not a punishment.

Rebellion invited death.
Obedience brings life.
The first Adam brought death.
The second Adam — **Jesus** — conquered it.

Romans 6:23 — *"For the wages of sin is death; but the gift
of God is eternal life through Jesus Christ our Lord."*

Closing Prayer

Lord, thank You for truth — even when it's weighty.
Help us not to treat sin lightly, knowing that it cost us our connection with You.
But thank You for Jesus, who faced death and defeated it.
Let us walk in obedience — not out of fear of death, but out of love for You.
Because of the cross, death no longer holds power over us.

In Jesus' name, Amen.

End of Bonus Episode

Next Time on Late Night with the Word...

It didn't move.
It didn't chase.
It didn't argue.
It just stood there — planted, waiting.

Next time, we talk to the **Tree of the Knowledge of Good and Evil.**
What was its purpose?
Was it set up as a trap or a test?
And why did God put it in the garden at all?

The answers may surprise you.

26

27

Episode 4: The Tree of the Knowledge of Good and Evil – The Silent Witness

Theme: *What do you do with the thing God says not to touch?*

Scripture: *Genesis 2:17 (KJV)* — "But of the tree of the knowledge of good and evil, thou shalt not eat of it: for in the day that thou eatest thereof thou shalt surely die."

Opening Monologue

It's funny how we remember what we're told *not* to do more than what we're told we *can* do.

You could be offered a hundred options, but the one thing off-limits?

That's the one you stare at.

In the middle of Eden stood a tree that didn't move, didn't speak, didn't chase or persuade.

Yet it held the weight of life and death.

It was a boundary — a line between trust and rebellion.

And though it never reached for Eve, somehow, it still became the center of the story.

Tonight, we're sitting down with a guest who never uttered a word but still carries the memory of a moment that changed everything.

Guest of the Night: The Tree of the Knowledge of Good and Evil – The Silent Witness

He didn't have roots of rebellion.

He stood in the middle of the most dangerous decision ever

28

made.

Please welcome — **The Tree of the Knowledge of Good and Evil!**

Host:

Welcome. You were planted in the middle of the garden. Did you know you would become such a focal point?

Tree:

I was placed with purpose. God planted me — not as a trap, but as a choice.

Every garden must have a boundary. Without it, love has no meaning.

Host:

You stood near the Tree of Life. Why do you think people focused on you more than the tree that offered eternal life?

Tree:

Because the human heart often craves what it can't have.

It's not that I was more powerful or more attractive — I represented what was withheld.

And what's withheld becomes desirable when trust fades.

Host:

So when Eve approached you, what did you feel?

Tree:

Grieved. Not because I had power, but because I had position.

I was the line.

When she reached out, I couldn't stop her.

I wasn't given arms to restrain — only presence, to remind them of God's command.

Host:

Why do you think God placed you there in the first place?

Tree:

Because without obedience, there is no relationship.

Love must be chosen. Trust must be tested.

I didn't bring death — disobedience did.

My presence gave them the chance to prove their devotion.

Host:

Do you regret being planted?

Tree:

No. I was a marker of divine trust.

My placement wasn't punishment — it was permission to grow in faith.

But when ignored, I became the line that was crossed.

And that crossroad changed everything.

The Big Truth

1. God Always Gives Permission Before He Gives Prohibition

Adam and Eve were told they could eat freely from *every other tree.*

Only one was off-limits.

God's nature is generous.

Boundaries protect — they don't restrict without reason.

2. Temptation Often Centers on Restriction, Not Blessing

The enemy drew Eve's attention to what was denied instead of what was freely given.

That's how temptation still works: it magnifies the *no* and makes you forget God's abundance.

3. Obedience Is Proof of Trust

The tree wasn't evil — the command was clear.
The presence of the tree gave Adam and Eve a daily chance to say, *"I trust God more than I trust my curiosity."*

4. The Test Wasn't About Fruit — It Was About Faith

What you reach for reveals what you believe.
Do you believe God is holding out on you, or holding you together?
Your decisions expose your doctrine.

5. Even Silence Has a Message

The tree didn't argue. It didn't resist.
But its presence preached a sermon: *Boundaries matter.*
And what God says matters more than what the serpent suggests.

Closing Prayer

I declare that I will not be drawn to what God has called forbidden.
I choose trust over curiosity, obedience over confusion, and faith over fear.
God's boundaries are for my good, and I will honor what He has commanded.

31

I will not be fooled by what looks pleasing but leads to death.

I stand planted in truth, and I will not be moved.

End of Episode 4

Next time on Late Night with the Word...

There's another tree in the garden — one that didn't bring death, but promised life.

We sit down with the **Tree of Life** and ask why it was ignored — and what it still offers us today.

33

Episode 5: The Tree of Life – The One That Still Offers Hope

Theme: *Life was always available. We just chose something else.*
Scripture: *Genesis 2:9 (KJV)* — "And out of the ground made the Lord God to grow every tree that is pleasant to the sight, and good for food; the tree of life also in the midst of the garden, and the tree of knowledge of good and evil."

Opening Monologue

Some things are so close, yet completely overlooked — like a gift sitting in the middle of the room while everyone stares at the one thing they can't touch.

In the center of Eden stood two trees. One brought consequence. The other offered life. But only one was chosen.

The Tree of Life never argued. Never demanded attention. It simply stood in its place, waiting for someone to choose what was already theirs.
It didn't tempt. It didn't shout. It just stood — as a promise of what could be.

Tonight, we welcome the One that still stands — in Scripture, in eternity, and in invitation.

Guest of the Night: The Tree of Life – The One That Still Offers Hope

She was planted with purpose and stood in the same garden that witnessed both creation and collapse.

34

Please welcome — **The Tree of Life!**

Host:
Thank you for joining us. You were there from the very beginning, yet you don't get talked about as much. Why do you think that is?

Tree of Life:
Because people often focus on what they've lost instead of what was always available.
While all eyes were on what was forbidden, I remained ready to give what was eternal.

Host:
You were in the same garden as the Tree of the Knowledge of Good and Evil. What was that dynamic like?

Tree of Life:
We stood together. One was the test. I was the reward.
I wasn't there to compete.
I was there to offer something lasting — uninterrupted fellowship, continual renewal, and the sustaining power of God's presence.

Host:
After the fall, Scripture says Adam and Eve were driven out and a flaming sword was placed to guard you. Why?

Tree of Life:
Because access to life must come through redemption, not rebellion.
If they had eaten from me after sinning, they would have lived forever in a broken state.
The sword was not rejection — it was protection.

Host:
So is your work done? Or are you still part of the story?

Tree of Life:
I am still part of the story. You'll find me again in Revelation.
I'm still standing. Still rooted. Still offering healing to the nations.
What was once guarded is now granted through the Lamb.

Host:
What do you want people to understand about you?

Tree of Life:
That life was always God's goal. Death was never His plan.
Every day in that garden, I stood as a reminder that His desire was not just creation — it was communion.

The Big Truth

1. God Never Removed Life. He Removed Access to Preserve Redemption.

The Tree of Life was not destroyed. It was guarded.
God's intention was never to cut off hope but to make room for grace.

2. Life Is Not Something You Earn. It's Something You Choose.

Adam and Eve had access to life but chose knowledge.
Many of us do the same: God offers peace, but we chase control.
He offers rest, but we reach for reason.

Choose life.

3. Redemption Protects What Rebellion Cannot Reach.

The flaming sword was not just judgment. It was mercy.
God knew that eternal life in a fallen state would be torment.
So He guarded what He plans to restore.

4. The Tree of Life Is Not Gone. It Is Waiting.

Revelation 22 says the Tree of Life will yield twelve kinds
of fruit and bring healing to the nations.
That means your future still holds hope, restoration, and
wholeness.

5. God's Presence Is the Real Fruit.

The Tree of Life wasn't just about immortality — it was
about intimacy.
To eat from it was to stay in step with the presence of God.
And that invitation still stands.

Closing Prayer

I declare that life is still available to me.
I will not be deceived into reaching for what leads to death.
I choose what God has always offered — His presence, His
promise, and His peace.

The Tree of Life still stands, and I stand with it.
What Adam lost, Christ restored.
I will live again.

End of Episode 5

Next time on Late Night with the Word...
Not everything that speaks is speaking truth.
The serpent enters the scene.
And for the first time, deception has a voice.

You don't want to miss it.

39

Episode 6: Host & Satan

Theme: *He didn't need a sword—just a sentence.*
Scripture: *Genesis 3:1 (KJV)* — "Yea, hath God said?"

Opening Monologue

Tonight's guest is the reason we have pain, pride, division, deception, and drama.
He was kicked out of heaven for trying to take the throne, and ever since, he's been trying to pull everyone else down with him.

He didn't use a knife in the garden—he used a question.
He didn't need force—he just needed to make Eve doubt.

If you're waiting for the devil to show up in red with horns, you're already behind.
His greatest weapon? **Subtlety.**

Let's bring him out—not to listen, but to learn how to fight.
Here he is: the deceiver, the accuser, the father of lies—
Satan.

Interview: Host × Satan

Host:
Let's be clear—this isn't a friendly welcome.
But we've got questions, and it's time we shine a light on your tricks.

Satan:
You can call it what you want.
I prefer *influence. Suggestion. Opportunity.*

40

Host:

Let's talk about that moment in Eden.
You didn't show up with thunder—you showed up with a whisper.

Satan:

Exactly. I don't need noise. I just need doubt.
All I said was, *"Did God really say that?"* That's it.
Just enough to shift her focus.
Just enough to twist the truth.

Host:

You knew the command, though. You knew God said not to eat from that tree.

Satan:

Of course. I know Scripture—I just prefer to bend it.

Host:

So you didn't attack Eve. You influenced her.

Satan:

She already had the Word, but I made her question it.
I made her think God was holding something back.
That's the secret: I didn't force her hand—I planted a thought.

Host:

Let's be honest—Eve didn't fall because of temptation. She fell because of twisted truth.

Satan:

Bingo.
I didn't lie outright; I reworded.
I distorted.
I wrapped deception in a little logic—and she dropped her

41

guard.

Host:

But you still lost. Because even after the fall, God made a promise.

Satan:

(Growls slightly) Yes… "Her seed will crush your head." I hate that part.

Host:

And that seed was Jesus—the Word made flesh.
The same Word that shuts you down every time.

Satan:

I don't mind emotions. I don't mind religion.
But when someone uses *the Word*—the real Word—I lose.

Host:

Exactly. That's the strategy.
You don't flee from feelings.
You flee from truth.
From *"It is written."*

The Big Truth

1. You Can't Fight the Devil Without the Word

The devil didn't win because he was stronger.
He influenced Eve because she didn't respond with the Word.

2. Satan's Greatest Weapon Is Deception

Genesis 3:1 — "Yea, hath God said?"
He doesn't usually push—he persuades.
He makes you question what God already told you.
He speaks just enough truth to sneak in a lie.
2 Corinthians 11:3 (KJV) — "The serpent beguiled Eve through his subtilty."

3. Your Feelings Are Not Your Shield—The Word Is

When Jesus was tempted in the wilderness (*Matthew 4*),
He didn't argue. He didn't reason.
He said, *"It is written."*

Eve knew the command, but she didn't declare it.
Jesus quoted the Word—and the devil had no choice but to flee.
James 4:7 (KJV) — "Resist the devil, and he will flee from you."

You don't resist him with tears or talk—you resist with truth.

4. Doubt Is the Door Satan Uses Most

Do you think he's going to tempt you with something obvious?
No. He comes in with:

"Are you sure God said that?"

"Does it really take all that?"

"What if He's holding back?"

43

Doubt is the seed.
Disobedience is the fruit.

5. You Can Shut Him Down Every Time with the Word

The Word isn't just a book—it's a weapon.
Ephesians 6:17 — "The sword of the Spirit, which is the Word of God."

When the enemy comes to deceive, distract, or discourage, the only thing that cuts through his lies is Scripture.

Prayer

Father, Thank You for exposing the tactics of the enemy.
I see now that the devil doesn't come loud—he comes subtle.
He doesn't push—he persuades.
And I won't be fooled.

Help me to hide Your Word in my heart so I won't sin against You.
Teach me to recognize the voice of the serpent and silence it with Scripture.
Give me wisdom and discernment to know when truth is being twisted.

And Lord, when temptation comes,
help me to respond the way Jesus did—with *"It is written."*
Let Your Word be my weapon.
Let Your truth be my shield.
And remind me daily that *greater is He that is in me than he that is in the world.*

In Jesus' name, Amen.

End of Episode 6

The serpent spoke, and the fall began.
But even in judgment, God's mercy moved.

He did not leave Adam and Eve without a future.
He covered them. He clothed them.
And He blocked the way to eternal separation.

Because love doesn't just give access—it also sets up guards.

Next time on Late Night with the Word...
We meet the angel assigned to stand watch.
With a flaming sword in hand, this messenger wasn't just guarding a tree—
he was holding the line between what was lost and what would one day be restored.

Don't miss it.

Episode 7: The Angel and the Sword – The Guardians of What's Still Holy

Theme: *Sometimes what looks like denial is actually divine protection.*

Scripture: *Genesis 3:24 (KJV)* — "So he drove out the man; and he placed at the east of the garden of Eden Cherubims, and a flaming sword which turned every way, to keep the way of the tree of life."

Opening Monologue

We don't always like to be told "no."
Especially when we're standing close to something that once belonged to us.

But what if that *no* wasn't rejection?
What if it was mercy standing in the gap with a flaming sword?

When Adam and Eve were sent out of the garden, it wasn't because God stopped loving them.
It was because love wouldn't let them stay broken forever.

To protect the future, God stationed a guard — not to keep them away from grace, but to prepare the way for it.

Tonight, we sit down with the angel who stood at the gate and the flame that never flickered out.

Guest of the Night: The Angel and the Sword – The Guardians of What's Still Holy

They weren't there to punish.

They were there to preserve.

Please welcome — **the Cherubim and the Flaming Sword.**

Host:

Angel, welcome. You were placed at the east of Eden with a sword that turned every way. What was your assignment?

Angel:

To protect what remained sacred.

The Tree of Life was never taken — it was guarded.

My role was not wrath. It was reverence.

I stood between what man wanted and what man could not handle in his fallen state.

Host:

Many people see the sword and assume anger.

Was this God's way of locking man out?

Angel:

No. It was His way of preparing the world for something better.

If Adam and Eve had eaten from the Tree of Life after sinning, they would have lived forever in a broken condition.

The sword was *mercy in motion.*

Host:

And the flame — was it literal or symbolic?

Angel:

Both. It was visible fire, yes, but it also represented the holiness of God.

Fire reveals, consumes, and purifies.

This flame was not fueled by judgment — it was lit by love.

48

Host:
So what were you really guarding — a tree, or something more?

Angel:
I was guarding *the way.*
The path back to life — the same way that one day would be opened again.
Not by sword, but by a cross.

Host:
Do you still stand watch today?

Angel:
Not in Eden. That moment passed.
But every time someone tries to come to God through works instead of grace, the sword still speaks.
Life is not earned.
It is accessed through the blood of the Lamb.

The Big Truth

1. God's "No" Is Not Rejection — It Is Redirection.

When God drove Adam and Eve out, it wasn't the end of the story.
It was the start of salvation.
The angel and the sword weren't barriers — they were boundaries of mercy.

2. Holiness Must Still Be Guarded.

The Tree of Life was holy.
God did not let fallen man treat the sacred like it was

common.
Even now, the things of God should not be handled lightly.
Some doors require reverence.

3. Divine Protection Often Looks Like Personal Denial.

We want what feels good; God gives what heals.
The sword wasn't meant to harm Adam and Eve — it was to
keep them from living forever in pain.
That's love.

4. The Sword Turned Every Way — Grace Would Reach Every Place.

No direction was missed.
No path was left unguarded.
The full circle of redemption was set in motion that day —
north, south, east, and west.
Salvation would be for *all* people.

5. God Never Stopped Guarding Life — He Just Changed the Access Point.

The gate was not closed forever.
It was waiting for Christ.
And once the veil tore, the way to life was no longer through
a guarded garden — it was through a risen Savior.

Closing Prayer

I declare that God's protection surrounds me, even when I

do not understand it.
I trust His boundaries.
I honor His holiness.
I believe the way to life has been opened through Jesus.

What was once guarded is now given.
I don't come by effort — I come by grace.
The fire still burns, but now it welcomes.
I will live by what He has provided.

End of Episode 7

Coming up next on Late Night with the Word...
From birthright to bloodshed, we sit down with the man who gave the first offering — and committed the first murder.

Jealousy opened the door, and sin was waiting.
Cain joins us on the couch.

Let's talk anger, offering, and the danger of ignoring God's warning.

Episode 8: Host & Cain

Theme: *When you let jealousy fester, it'll turn your hands into weapons.*
Scripture: *Genesis 4:7 (KJV)* — "Sin lieth at the door. And unto thee shall be his desire, and thou shalt rule over him."

Opening Monologue

Tonight's guest is known for something heavy.
His name is marked in history — not for invention, not for wisdom, but for being the first to ever take a life.

But before the blood, there was bitterness.
Before the murder, there was a missed moment with God.

Cain didn't fall because God hated him.
Cain fell because he didn't deal with what was happening inside of him.

This is more than a story about murder — it's a story about jealousy, pride, and a God who tried to step in before it went too far.

Let's dig in.
Put your hands together — he's walking out of history and into the studio.
Cain, welcome to the couch.

Interview: Host × Cain

Host:
Cain — firstborn of Adam and Eve. Let's talk.
Everyone knows what you did, but I want to talk about what you felt.
Let's rewind.

Cain:
(Sighs) It started with a seed — jealousy.
My brother Abel and I both brought offerings to God.
I gave fruit from the ground; he brought the best from his flock.
God accepted his — but not mine.

Host:
Did God say He hated your offering?

Cain:
No. That's the thing.
He didn't curse me. He didn't scream at me.
He just didn't receive it with favor — and it stung.
But instead of humbling myself, I got heated.

Host:
And God actually warned you, right?

Cain:
Yeah. He said, *"Why are you angry? If you do well, shall you not be accepted?"*
Then He said something that still echoes in me: *"Sin is lying at your door, but you must rule over it."*

Host:
So you had a choice.

Cain:

I did. But I let the anger fester.

I looked at Abel like the enemy when the real enemy was inside me.

One day, I invited him to the field. No argument. No heads-up. Just rage.

I struck him — and just like that, my brother was gone.

Host:

And then?

Cain:

God came — like He always does.

Not to kill me, but to hold me accountable.

He asked me, *"Where is your brother?"* And I lied.

I said, *"Am I my brother's keeper?"* But I knew.

Host:

How did God respond?

Cain:

He didn't destroy me.

He marked me — not to curse me, but to protect me.

That's the part people miss.

Even after what I did, He still put something on me to let others know: *Don't touch him.*

That mark was mercy.

The Big Truth

You Can't Worship While Hiding Bitterness

Cain teaches us something we all need to hear:
Unchecked emotions turn into unholy actions.

1. God Wants Your Heart, Not Just Your Hand

Genesis 4:4-5 — "And the Lord had respect unto Abel and to his offering: But unto Cain and to his offering he had not respect."
God didn't reject Cain — He rejected the condition of the offering.
Cain brought something, but it wasn't his best.
It wasn't from the heart.

2. Sin Doesn't Kick the Door Down — It Waits for You to Open It

Genesis 4:7 — "Sin lieth at the door."
God warned him.
Sin was crouching like a lion, ready to pounce.
But God also said: *"You must rule over it."*
Translation: You've got authority — but you've got to use it.

3. Your Real Fight Is Internal

Cain's enemy wasn't Abel — it was his own pride, jealousy, and offense.
It's easy to point outward, but the battle always starts within.

4. God Still Shows Mercy — Even After Our Worst

Cain's judgment was real, but so was the mark.
God marked him — not to shame him, but to show He still had purpose even in punishment.

Genesis 4:15 — "And the Lord set a mark upon Cain, lest any finding him should kill him."

Prayer

Father,
Help me to recognize the emotions that crouch at my door.
When jealousy rises, help me shut it down.
When bitterness creeps in, let me confront it before it grows.

I don't want to worship with the wrong heart.
I don't want to bring You offerings without bringing You obedience.

Lord, help me master what's trying to master me.
Let me rule over what wants to ruin me.

And when I fall, remind me that Your mercy still marks me
— not to condemn, but to call me higher.

In Jesus' name, Amen.

End of Episode 8

Next time on Late Night with the Word...
It wasn't a tattoo. It wasn't a scar for decoration.
It was a divine mark — placed by God, not to punish, but to protect.

Cain's actions cried out from the ground,
but his mark spoke of mercy.

In this **bonus episode**, we interview the **Mark of Cain** itself.
What did it feel like to carry the weight of consequence and

57

the covering of compassion?

Let's find out.

Bonus Episode: Cain's Scar — The Mark That Spoke

Theme: *God's mercy can still mark you, even when you've messed up.*
Genesis 4:15 (KJV) *"And the Lord set a mark upon Cain, lest any finding him should kill him."*

Opening Monologue

Some scars are silent. Others scream.
But every now and then, a scar speaks.

Cain was the firstborn man. The first to work the ground.
The first to bring an offering.
And the first to commit murder.

After killing his brother Abel, God confronted him—but what came next wasn't total destruction. It was a mark.

Tonight, we speak to that scar: a permanent reminder not just of Cain's guilt, but of God's protection.

Guest of the Night: Cain's Scar

Host:
Tonight's guest is not a person, but a proof.
It didn't bleed, but it never disappeared.
Please welcome the symbol of God's mercy and memory—

Cain's Scar.

Scar:
I was never meant to glamorize what he did.
I was meant to warn others—and protect him—all at once.

60

Host:

Let's start with that. What exactly are you?

Scar:

I'm a mark. A divine appointment of mercy.

When Cain cried out, afraid that people would kill him in retaliation, God didn't ignore him.

Even after judgment, He gave protection.

Host:

But you're a scar. Don't scars mean pain?

Scar:

Yes. Pain happened. Innocence was lost.

But I don't just remind Cain of Abel's blood—I remind him of God's choice not to kill him.

That's mercy in visible form.

Host:

Did Cain ever try to cover you up?

Scar:

Of course. Shame always wants to hide what God uses to teach.

But over time, he realized I wasn't just punishment—I was promise.

A reminder that God would still watch over him, even in exile.

Host:

Some might say you're a symbol of failure.

Scar:

I'm a symbol of consequence, yes—but also of restraint.

Cain deserved more, but God gave less.

That's grace. Not freedom to sin again, but a shield against

61

total destruction.

Host:
What would you say to people who are living with scars today?

Scar:
You don't have to let shame define you.
Let the scar remind you—not of your sin, but of the God who saw your worst and didn't walk away.
Some marks aren't meant to haunt you; they're meant to humble you.

The Big Truth

God doesn't erase all scars—sometimes He leaves them as a mercy.

Cain's scar wasn't an endorsement of sin; it was protection from vengeance.

Even after judgment, God still listens to the cry of the guilty.

Your scars can speak of the grace that held you together when you should've fallen apart.

Psalm 103:10 — *"He hath not dealt with us after our sins; nor rewarded us according to our iniquities."*
Lamentations 3:22 — *"It is of the Lord's mercies that we are not consumed."*

Closing Prayer

Lord,
Thank You for mercy I didn't deserve.

Even when I fell, You didn't let destruction have the final word.
Thank You for the scars that remind me of grace, not just guilt.
Help me walk humbly, live wisely, and never forget the mercy that marked me.
In Jesus' name, Amen.

End of Bonus Episode.

Coming up next on Late Night with the Word

He didn't say much, but his worship spoke volumes.
His sacrifice pleased God, and his blood still speaks.

Abel steps into the spotlight.
Let's talk obedience, offering, and what true worship really looks like.

Episode 9: Host & Abel

Theme: *You don't have to be loud to be heard by heaven.*
Scripture: *Hebrews 11:4 (KJV)* — "He being dead yet speaketh."

Opening Monologue

Tonight's guest didn't build a boat, lead a nation, or write any psalms.
He's not known for words — but for *worship.*

He brought something simple, yet it had substance.
He gave from the heart, and God took notice.
His brother brought fruit, but he brought *faith.*

His story is short, but it's loud in the spirit.
And though his brother tried to silence him, his blood still speaks.

Tonight, we're honoring the first worshipper who made heaven stand up.
Give it up for **Abel.**

Interview: Host × Abel

Host:
Abel, welcome to the show. You may not have said a lot in *Genesis,* but man — your actions are still echoing.

Abel:
Thank you. It's not about how much I said — it's about what I gave.

65

Host:

Let's jump in. Walk us through that moment — you and your brother Cain, both bringing offerings to the Lord.

Abel:

It was simple. I brought the firstlings of my flock — the best of the firstborn.

Not just any sheep, but a blood sacrifice. That's what God required.

Without blood, there's no covering. No atonement.

Host:

So your offering wasn't just about generosity — it was about obedience.

Abel:

Exactly. Cain brought what he *wanted*. I brought what God *asked* for.

He gave from the ground, but God had already cursed the ground in *Genesis 3*.

Fruit can't cover sin. Blood had to be shed. That was God's standard from the beginning.

Host:

Whewww. So even then, the blood was speaking.

Abel:

It always has. God was showing us early on — it would take blood to deal with sin.

That pointed forward to the ultimate sacrifice: Jesus, the Lamb of God.

Host:

But when God accepted your offering...

Abel:

66

My brother's face changed.
He didn't say it, but I saw it — offense, jealousy, rage.

Host:
And that led to the field.

Abel:
Yeah. But even in death, God didn't forget.
My blood still spoke — not revenge, but remembrance.

The Big Truth

Abel's life teaches us that God doesn't just see *what* you bring — He sees *why* you bring it.

1. God Looks at the Heart, Not Just the Hands

Genesis 4:4 (KJV) — "And the Lord had respect unto Abel and to his offering."
Cain brought fruit. Abel brought his first and best.
God doesn't just want what's easy — He wants what's honest.

2. Worship That Costs Nothing Means Nothing

Abel didn't give leftovers; he gave sacrifice.
His offering hurt a little — but it honored a lot.
2 Samuel 24:24 (KJV) — "I will not offer that which doth cost me nothing."
God receives what reflects *faith,* not just function.

3. Jealousy Is a Spirit That Targets the Favored

Abel didn't provoke Cain — his obedience did.
Be careful: sometimes your worship exposes someone else's rebellion.

4. Your Worship Can Outlive You

Hebrews 11:4 — "By faith Abel offered… and by it he being dead yet speaketh."
Even though Abel died, his offering lives.
When your worship is real, it keeps talking long after you stop.

5. Abel's Blood Pointed to Jesus' Blood

Abel's sacrifice wasn't random — it was prophetic.
Genesis 4:4 — "And Abel brought of the firstlings of his flock."

From the very beginning, God showed that blood was required to cover sin.
After Adam and Eve fell, God didn't cover them with fig leaves — He clothed them with animal skins (*Genesis 3:21*).
That was the first blood sacrifice.

Abel followed that pattern.
His offering wasn't just about giving — it was about obedience to God's standard of a blood covering.

Hebrews 9:22 (KJV) — "Without shedding of blood is no remission [of sin]."
His sacrifice was a shadow of the Savior to come.

Hebrews 12:24 (KJV) — "…and to the blood of sprinkling, that speaketh better things than that of Abel."

Abel's blood cried out from the ground.
But Jesus' blood cried out from the cross: *"It is finished."*

Abel's worship cost him everything.
But Jesus' sacrifice paid for everything.

Prayer

Father,
Thank You for teaching me through Abel's story that true worship comes from the heart — that obedience matters more than performance.
You weren't just looking for a gift; You were looking for faith and sacrifice.

Thank You for revealing that blood was always Your standard — not because You delight in death,
but because You made a way for covering, mercy, and redemption.

Help me to bring You not just what's easy, but what's holy.
Not just what looks good, but what You asked for.

And thank You for the ultimate sacrifice — Jesus, the Lamb of God,
whose blood speaks better things than Abel's ever could.

Let my life be an offering.
Let my obedience speak.
And when I worship, let it reflect the cross — not just my voice.

In Jesus' name, Amen.

69

End of Episode 9

Blood cried out. Judgment fell.
A brother's hands became the evidence of a heart turned away from God.

But while Cain walked away marked, something else remained behind — the ground.

It received the blood.
It absorbed the curse.
It carried the consequences.

Next time on Late Night with the Word...
We hear from the one thing beneath it all.
The ground speaks — it remembers what fell on it, what grew from it, and what was taken from it.

You won't want to miss **Episode 10: The Ground – Cursed After the Fall, Then Soaked by Abel's Blood.**

71

Episode 10: The Ground – Cursed After the Fall, Then Soaked by Abel's Blood

Theme: *What you cover, I carry. What you kill, I remember.*
Scripture: *Genesis 4:10-11 (KJV)* — "And he said, What hast thou done? the voice of thy brother's blood crieth unto me from the ground. And now art thou cursed from the earth, which hath opened her mouth to receive thy brother's blood from thy hand."

Opening Monologue

Most people overlook the ground.
We walk on it. Build on it. Bury things in it.
But tonight — the ground gets a voice.

It's easy to talk about Cain and Abel:
one gave the right offering, the other gave what was easy.
One pleased God, the other got jealous.

But after the murder, God didn't speak to Cain first about his heart — He spoke about *the ground.*

Because the ground didn't just catch Abel's body — it caught his blood.
And blood doesn't die quietly.

Tonight, we hear from the one who has held every seed, every footprint, and every drop of spilled truth since the beginning.

Guest of the Night: The Ground – The Silent Record Keeper

You've walked over it. You've buried things in it.
But you've never heard it speak — until now.

Please welcome **The Ground.**

Host:
Welcome. You were there in the beginning — formed by
God, holding the first breath of man.
What do you remember?

Ground:
I remember purity. Peace. Purpose.
I remember Adam formed from my dust, and God breathing
into him.
I was not just a floor — I was a foundation for fellowship.

Host:
But after the fall, things changed.
How did you feel when the curse came?

Ground:
I felt it deeply.
The weight of rebellion sank into me.
Thorns and thistles began to grow.
What once responded to beauty now responded to
brokenness.
I was cursed because man disobeyed.
I didn't eat the fruit — but I bore the result.

Host:
And then came Abel — the first man to die.
What happened when his blood touched you?

Ground:
I opened up.
I didn't just receive his blood — I listened to it.
Because blood speaks.

His blood cried out with a voice heaven could not ignore.
I could not cover it.
I could not silence it.
I could only hold the sound of injustice.

Host:
God said Cain was cursed from the earth.
What did that mean?

Ground:
It meant I would no longer give him increase.
He poured death into me; I could no longer pour life into him.
A cursed heart cannot pull blessing from a cursed place.

Host:
What do you carry now?

Ground:
I carry memory.
I carry stories.
I carry seeds and secrets — every drop of blood spilled in violence, every prayer whispered in the soil, every harvest and famine.
I hold it all.
But I also wait.
I wait for the day when there will be no more curse.

The Big Truth

1. The Ground Is Not Just Soil — It Is a Witness.

What is buried is not always silent.
Abel's blood cried out from the ground, and God heard it.

Nothing is truly hidden when heaven is listening.

2. Sin Doesn't Just Affect the Heart — It Changes the Environment.

The ground was cursed because of Adam, then it was shut to Cain.
What you do in secret often shows up in what refuses to grow.

3. God Listens to What We Try to Bury.

Abel's death was meant to be covered, but God listens to blood.
He hears what we pretend to silence.
His justice is never blind.

4. You Can't Harvest Life from Cursed Soil.

Cain wanted increase from the earth after giving it death.
But the ground shut down — the same way your future shuts down when you sow into it with disobedience.

5. Jesus' Blood Speaks Better Things.

The Book of Hebrews says that the blood of Jesus speaks better than that of Abel.
One cried for justice — the other declares mercy.
What was once cursed will be restored by the One who bled for us all.

75

Closing Prayer

I declare that what I have buried will not go unheard.
God sees, God knows, and God remembers.
I release every hidden thing into His hands.

I will not sow death and expect life.
I ask for mercy where there was once silence.
I believe that the blood of Jesus still speaks, still cleanses,
and still restores.
And because of that, I will live free.

End of Episode 10

Coming up next on Late Night with the Word...
He didn't build an ark. He didn't part a sea.
He just walked so closely with God that he never saw death.

Enoch is stepping into the studio.
Let's talk intimacy, legacy, and what it means to walk with
God until the world loses sight of you.

77

Episode 11: Host & Enoch

Theme: *When you walk with God daily, disappearing doesn't mean you're lost — it means you're with Him.*
Scripture: *Genesis 5:24 (KJV)* — "And Enoch walked with God: and he was not; for God took him."

Opening Monologue

Tonight's guest isn't known for miracles, battles, or building big things.
You won't find a long speech from him or any dramatic scenes — but you will find one sentence that shook heaven and inspired generations:

Enoch walked with God.

No crowds. No titles.
Just a quiet, consistent, unshakable walk.

He didn't chase platforms — he chased presence.
And one day, the walk got so deep, God said, *"You don't have to go back."*

Tonight, let's welcome the man who skipped death and stepped into eternity.
Enoch is in the studio.

Interview: Host × Enoch

Host:
Enoch, welcome to the show. I'm gonna be real — you've got one of the shortest bios in *Genesis,* but one of the strongest impacts.

78

Enoch:
That's the goal. I wasn't living to be remembered by earth — I was walking to be known in heaven.

Host:
Talk to us about that. What does it mean to walk with God?

Enoch:
It means agreement.
It means I didn't just visit Him on the Sabbath — I walked with Him in my everyday.
I asked Him what He thought. I listened. I aligned. I surrendered.
I wasn't perfect — but I was present.

Host:
You weren't a king, a priest, or a prophet. You were just…

Enoch:
…just consistent.
In a world growing darker by the day, I chose to walk in light.
I wasn't trying to be famous — I was trying to stay close.

Host:
Then one day, you were gone.

Enoch:
Yes. I felt the pull stronger than usual.
God didn't say much — He just took me.
One moment I was walking on earth, and the next, I was walking in glory.

Host:
Death never touched you.

79

Enoch:
No. Because when your walk is right, death becomes just a doorway — and God is the One waiting on the other side.

The Big Truth

1. God Notices Who Walks With Him

Genesis 5:24 — "And Enoch walked with God: and he was not; for God took him."
He wasn't taken because he was special — he was taken because he was faithful.
God doesn't just want your moments; He wants your movement with Him.

2. Faithful Obedience Over Time Is What Moves Heaven

Hebrews 11:5 — "By faith Enoch was translated that he should not see death… for before his translation he had this testimony, that he pleased God."
You don't have to do big things to please God.
Just walk. Just obey. Just stay in rhythm with Him.

3. The World May Lose Sight of You When You're Hidden in God

Enoch "was not" — people couldn't find him.
When you walk with God, don't be surprised if the world loses its grip on you.
Sometimes walking with God means disappearing from places that no longer feed your spirit.

4. Walking With God Is the Ultimate Goal

Not titles. Not followers. Not applause. Just *Him.*
Enoch teaches us that the real reward isn't what we get on earth — it's *who* we walk with every day.

Prayer

Father,
Teach me how to walk with You like Enoch did — not just in public, but in private.
Not just in church, but in my everyday.

Let my life be a steady rhythm of obedience, worship, and trust.
When others are chasing platforms, let me chase Your presence.
When the world gets louder, help me tune my ear to Your voice.

And if the road gets lonely, remind me that I'm never walking alone.
Let my consistency be my calling card.
Let my faith be my legacy.

In Jesus' name, Amen.

End of Episode 11

Up next on Late Night with the Word...
He watched generations rise and fall.
He lived nearly a thousand years, but his name carried a

prophecy.

Methuselah is on the way.
Let's talk **time, timing,** and how a life can become a countdown to something greater.

Episode 12: Host & Methuselah

Theme: *God knows how to wait, and sometimes your life is the warning before the rain.*
Scripture: *Genesis 5:27 (KJV)* — "And all the days of Methuselah were nine hundred sixty and nine years: and he died."

Opening Monologue

Tonight's guest is the oldest man to ever live — and probably the only person who ever celebrated his 900th birthday with a party *and* a prayer meeting!

Let's be real — when you've lived that long?
His first cellphone was two rocks and a carrier dove.

He's the only man who saw the world go from fire pits to Wi-Fi.
He didn't just live through history — he proofread it.
When he says *"back in my day,"* he means *Genesis*.

But Methuselah isn't just known for how long he lived.
He's known for what his life represented.
His name carried a countdown — and when he died, the rain began.

Let's welcome the man with more candles than cake —
Methuselah!

Interview: Host × Methuselah

Host:
Sir Methuselah, what an honor. 969 years old — you look

84

good!

Methuselah:
(Laughs) Moisturize with olive oil and mind your business. It works.

Host:
You lived longer than anybody on record. What was your secret?

Methuselah:
Simple. Walk with God, mind your lane, and don't stress. I had more time than most because my life was tied to something bigger than me.

Host:
Let's talk about that. You weren't just a long-liver — you were a living prophecy.
Your name literally means *"When he dies, it shall come."* What did that mean to you?

Methuselah:
My father Enoch told me, *"Your life is a countdown. As long as you live, judgment waits. But when you go, the rain will fall."*
Every birthday, I wasn't just getting older — I was holding back a flood.

Host:
So your death was connected to the flood in Noah's time?

Methuselah:
Exactly. I died the same year the rain started.
My life was God's mercy clock ticking — giving people time to repent.

Host:

You saw generations pass. What was that like?

Methuselah:

I watched people rise and fall.
I buried sons, grandsons, great-great-greats — it was heavy.
But I also saw God's patience.
I was proof that He delays judgment — not because He's soft, but because He's merciful.

Host:

Would you say your life was about waiting?

Methuselah:

It was about warning.
I was a living grace period.
But people ignored it. They laughed, they partied, they mocked Noah —
and the whole time, my breath was God's way of saying,
"I'm still giving you time."

The Big Truth

1. God's Mercy Has a Pulse

Genesis 5:27 — "...and he died."
That's when the flood came.
For 969 years, Methuselah's life held back the storm.
Some people are alive today not just for themselves —
but because their presence is holding open the door for someone else to repent.

2. Your Life Might Be the Clock Others Are Ignoring

People mocked Noah, but Methuselah's life was the countdown.
He was grace wrapped in age.

2 Peter 3:9 (KJV) — "The Lord is not slack concerning his promise, but is longsuffering to us-ward."
God's patience isn't delay — it's divine compassion.

3. Longevity Doesn't Always Equal Legacy

Methuselah lived the longest, but it's what his *name* meant that mattered most.
A long life is good — but a life that means something is better.

4. Don't Waste the Waiting

God gave the world almost 1,000 years of warning before the flood.
That wasn't delay — it was divine patience.
Don't waste the time He's giving you.

Isaiah 55:6 (KJV) — "Seek ye the Lord while He may be found, call ye upon Him while He is near."

Prayer

Father,
Thank You for showing me that time is not to be wasted.
If I'm still breathing, it means You still have purpose for me —

and patience for others through me.

Like Methuselah, help me to live a life that represents Your mercy.
Let my time be a testimony. Let my days carry meaning.

And if I'm someone else's window to see You —
don't let me block their view.

Use my life to delay destruction and extend Your grace.

In Jesus' name, Amen.

End of Episode 12

Next time on Late Night with the Word...
The skies were silent. The earth was wicked.
And one man picked up a hammer in obedience.

While others laughed, he measured.
While they partied, he prepared.

Noah is stepping into the studio.
Let's talk **faith, blueprints, obedience,**
and what it's like to be saved by something you built in private.

Episode 13: Host & Noah

Theme: *Sometimes faith looks like building when there's no sign of rain.*
Scripture: *Hebrews 11:7 (KJV)* — "By faith Noah, being warned of God of things not seen as yet, moved with fear, prepared an ark…"

Opening Monologue

Tonight's guest is the reason we're even having a show right now.
When the world went wild, he picked up a hammer.
When sin covered the earth, he covered the wood with pitch.

No one had ever seen rain, but God gave him a forecast that would change the world.
He believed before he saw.
He built before it made sense.
And while others laughed — he obeyed.

Get ready to meet the original survivor — the blueprint builder, the animal wrangler, the water-walking prepper himself…
Noah is in the studio!

Interview: Host × Noah

Host:
Noah! Finally — the man who built the ark. It's an honor to have you.

Noah:
Glad to be here. Been on water for a while — good to be

back on dry land.

Host:
Let's get right to it. You heard from God, and He told you to build a boat before rain was even a thing. What was that like?

Noah:
It was wild. I didn't even know what rain was.
But when God speaks, you don't wait for confirmation — you start cutting wood.
I had never seen a storm, but I trusted the Voice.

Host:
So He didn't just give you a word — He gave you measurements.

Noah:
Exactly. God is specific.
I wasn't just building a boat — I was building salvation.
He gave me dimensions, materials, even the number of floors.
He told me what to pitch it with.
Faith isn't random — it's structured obedience.

Host:
And while you built, people mocked.

Noah:
Every day. They called me crazy. Said I was wasting my life.
They laughed while I labored.
But what they didn't realize was: I wasn't building for the moment — I was building for what was coming.

Host:
Whew. And it took decades, right?

Noah:

Over a hundred years.

That's faith that works even when nothing changes.

Some mornings I felt doubt. Other days I felt discouraged.

But I kept building. Because God said it — and that was enough.

Host:

Then the day came…

Noah:

The sky cracked. The ground broke open.

Water fell from heaven and rose from below.

Suddenly, the mockers were missing — and the blueprint made sense.

Host:

And the door closed.

Noah:

Yes. God shut it — not me.

I didn't beg people to get on; I just obeyed.

That was the hardest part — knowing the door could have stayed open if they'd listened.

But when grace is rejected, judgment follows.

Host:

Any regrets?

Noah:

None. I obeyed. I warned. I worked. And I worshipped.

And when the rain stopped — I had a new beginning.

The Big Truth

Noah's story reminds us that faith is not just belief — it's *construction.*
You build what God says, even when it looks foolish.

1. Obedience Doesn't Wait for Evidence

Hebrews 11:7 — "Noah moved with fear, prepared an ark to the saving of his house."
There was no sign of rain. No thunder. No clouds.
Just God's word — and that was enough.

2. People Will Always Mock What They Don't Understand

Noah preached while he built — and they laughed.
But their laughter didn't stop the flood.
Rejection doesn't cancel the assignment.

3. Faith Requires Work

Noah didn't just believe — he built.
Day after day. In silence. In sweat. In the unknown.
James 2:17 — "Faith without works is dead."
God gave the word, but Noah grabbed the hammer.

4. God Will Always Close What He Opens — On His Terms

Genesis 7:16 — "And the Lord shut him in."

When God shuts the door, it's protection — not punishment.
Don't waste time trying to reopen what God has already
sealed.

5. What You Build in Faith Will Save You in the Flood

When you build in obedience, your survival is hidden in
your structure.
The ark wasn't just a boat — it was a promise on water.

Prayer

Father,
Thank You for Noah's faith — the kind that builds before it
sees.
Teach me to trust Your voice above the noise.

Help me to obey You even when people mock me.
Let me keep building, even when I'm tired.
Even when it looks crazy.
Even when I don't understand.

If You give the blueprint, I'll pick up the tools.
And when the rain comes, let me be found safe
in the thing I built by faith.

In Jesus' name, Amen.

End of Episode 13

Next time on Late Night with the Word...
She stood beside the man who built what no one believed in.
She endured the silence, the stares, the waiting, and the

waves.

Noah's wife takes the stage.
Let's talk **faith behind the scenes** — and what it means to hold the house while the ark is still being built.

Episode 14: Host & Noah's Wife

Theme: *She didn't need to be loud to be legendary.*
Scripture: *Genesis 7:7 (KJV)* — "And Noah went in, and his sons, and his wife…"

Opening Monologue

Tonight's guest doesn't have a famous speech.
She didn't build an altar or write a psalm.
Her name was never mentioned — but her presence was undeniable.

While Noah was hammering wood, she was holding down the home.
While he preached to people who ignored him, she raised sons who followed him.

She boarded the ark not because she had all the answers, but because she had enough faith to *stay.*

She is the blueprint for women who pray in silence,
obey in the shadows,
and believe in the God of their household — even when the world around them is falling apart.

Give it up for the original *First Lady of the Flood — Noah's wife is in the studio!*

Interview: Host × Noah's Wife

Host:
Mrs. Noah, welcome! So good to finally hear from the woman who helped carry the promise.

Noah's Wife:

Thank you. I don't mind that my name isn't recorded.
Sometimes your faith *is* your legacy.

Host:

Let's talk about it. What was it like being married to a man
building an ark before rain was ever a thing?

Noah's Wife:

It wasn't easy.
I watched my husband wake up every day and build
something no one believed in.
People laughed. Family distanced themselves.
It was lonely.
But I knew — if he was faithful to God, I had to be faithful
to him.

Host:

You were raising sons during this time. What was that like?

Noah's Wife:

I raised boys in a world headed for destruction.
I had to teach them how to obey even when they didn't
understand.
I told them, *"Your father hears from God, even when no one
else does."*
My job wasn't to preach — it was to protect their posture.

Host:

When the flood came, what were you feeling?

Noah's Wife:

Terror. Grief. Relief.
Everything we'd heard — everything Noah warned about —
it all came true.

But there was also peace.

Because we were inside what we built.

I stood beside him in the dry season so I could survive with him in the storm.

Host:

Whew. So powerful. Any final words to the silent women holding it all together?

Noah's Wife:

Yes. You don't have to be loud to be used.

Obedience echoes.

Faith behind the scenes still moves heaven.

Your *yes* in the shadows carries just as much power as the one on the platform.

And trust me — God sees it all.

The Big Truth

Noah gets the spotlight, but his wife carried stability.

She was the first woman to board the ark — and she didn't need applause to obey.

1. Faith Doesn't Always Speak — Sometimes It Stands

Genesis 7:7 — "…and Noah went in, and his sons, and his wife."

She didn't preach. She didn't prophesy.

She simply stood beside the promise.

99

2. Support Is Spiritual

Her support kept Noah steady.
While he built on the outside, she helped build the faith inside their home.
Sometimes, support is more powerful than a sermon.

3. You Don't Need a Platform to Walk in Purpose

She was part of the promise because she stayed connected to it.
God didn't ask her to build the ark,
but her presence was necessary for what came after.

4. God Sees Who Walks Beside the Builder

You may not be leading the vision,
but your loyalty is part of the assignment.
She was chosen — not just as Noah's wife,
but as a mother to the world that would start over.

Closing Prayer

Father,
Thank You for reminding me that You see the unseen.
That You honor silent faith, quiet strength, and behind-the-scenes obedience.

Help me to be faithful in the flood, not just the favor.
Let me walk beside what You're building,
even if I didn't hear the instructions myself.

Make me steady.

100

Make me supportive.
Make me secure in You — whether I'm named or not.

And when the storms come,
may I be found inside the obedience I helped carry.

In Jesus' name, Amen.

End of Episode 14

The flood was coming, but obedience got to work before the first drop ever fell.
Noah didn't just believe God — he built with every word God said, trusting in a plan that had never been tested before.

But there's one part of the story we haven't heard from yet: the vessel that held the future — the wooden walls that carried worship, water, and wonder.

Next time on Late Night with the Word...
We sit down with **the Ark.**
It was more than a boat — it was a symbol of salvation and obedience.
And now, for the first time, **the Ark speaks.**

Episode 15: The Ark – A Symbol of Salvation and Obedience

Theme: *When God gives you the blueprint, your obedience builds the rescue.*

Scripture: *Genesis 6:14 (KJV)* — "Make thee an ark of gopher wood; rooms shalt thou make in the ark, and shalt pitch it within and without with pitch."

Opening Monologue

Sometimes salvation doesn't come with wings or a bright light.
Sometimes it looks like a long stretch of wood — hammered by obedience, sealed with pitch, and floating on faith.

When judgment was about to rain down on the earth, God didn't just send a warning — He sent instructions.
And one man followed them with steady hands and a reverent heart.
But tonight, we're not just talking about the man — we're talking about what he built.

The Ark didn't speak a word.
It didn't preach.
It didn't beg.
It simply *stood* — rising plank by plank in a world that refused to listen.
And when the waters rose, it became what no one expected:
a lifeline.

Tonight, we interview a vessel that once held the future of the world inside its walls.

Guest of the Night: The Ark – A Symbol of Salvation and Obedience

It was made by man, designed by God, and trusted to float through judgment carrying everything that would restart creation.
Please welcome — **The Ark.**

Host:
Welcome, Ark. You didn't have a voice when you were built, but you sure had a purpose.
What do you remember most?

Ark:
I remember the silence — the sound of hammers over mockery, the smell of gopher wood soaked in pitch.
I remember obedience when no one else understood.

Host:
You were built to specific dimensions. Why did that matter?

Ark:
Because survival isn't based on creativity — it's based on obedience.
Every measurement was protection.
Every instruction was life.
When Noah followed God precisely, I became a safe place.

Host:
You carried animals, Noah, his family, and the future of the world. What was that like?

Ark:
Heavy — but holy.

I didn't choose who entered; God did.
I didn't shut the door; He did.
But once they were inside, I became the shelter that held covenant, legacy, and promise.

Host:
Many probably saw you as just a boat. Were you more than that?

Ark:
Much more.
I was a symbol — a line between judgment and mercy.
I did not sail with speed; I *stood* with purpose.
My strength wasn't in my shape — it was in the Word that commanded me to exist.

Host:
When the rains stopped and the ground dried, did you feel your purpose was finished?

Ark:
No.
My floating ended, but my meaning continued.
I was a testimony of what happens when people obey before they understand.
I was a picture of Christ before they ever knew His name.

The Big Truth

1. The Ark Was Not a Reaction — It Was a Response to Obedience

God didn't build the Ark — Noah did, because he obeyed.
Obedience makes room for rescue.

When God speaks, your response can become someone else's survival.

2. You Don't Need a Crowd to Confirm What God Told You to Build

Noah had no applause — just instructions.
Faith is proven in the process, not the platform.
The Ark was built in silence before it stood in significance.

3. Judgment May Fall, but Obedience Floats

The same water that destroyed the earth lifted the Ark.
What drowned others carried Noah to safety.
Your obedience will carry you when the storm hits.

4. The Door Was Shut by God

Noah didn't close it — God did.
That was divine timing.
Some opportunities are not for man to manage.
When God says the time is up, He seals what He has chosen.

5. The Ark Is a Shadow of Christ

One way in. One door. One shelter. Just like Jesus.
Those who were inside were saved — not because of their strength,
but because they trusted the only place of protection provided.

Closing Prayer

I declare that I will build what God gives me, even if the world does not understand it.
I will not wait for rain to believe the warning.
I choose obedience over approval.

What I build in private will be used for purpose.
The same God who gave Noah the blueprint is giving me the grace to complete mine.

I will walk in the shelter of His Word — and I will live.

In Jesus' name, Amen.

End of Episode 15

The waters rose. The Ark lifted. The door was shut.
Now the storm speaks.

Next time on Late Night with the Word...
We listen to **the voice of the Flood** itself — to ask what it saw, what it broke, and what it buried.

Episode 16: The Flood – The Storm That Obeyed God's Voice

Theme: *When God speaks, even the waters listen.*
Scripture: *Genesis 7:11-12 (KJV)* — "...the same day were all the fountains of the great deep broken up, and the windows of heaven were opened. And the rain was upon the earth forty days and forty nights."

Opening Monologue

Some storms come out of nowhere.
Others are announced long before the sky ever darkens.

This one didn't sneak in. It was prophesied, measured, and sent on assignment.
The Flood wasn't random. It didn't come to ruin what was good—
it came to wash away what refused to change.

For forty days and forty nights the heavens opened,
the deep broke loose, and the ground trembled under judgment.
But the rain wasn't the enemy.
The disobedience that called it forth was.

Tonight, we interview the Flood—
not as chaos, but as a servant of God that answered His command and kept His timing.

Guest of the Night: The Flood – The Storm That Obeyed God's Voice

It wasn't driven by nature.

109

It was sent by the Creator.

Please welcome — **The Flood.**

Host:

Welcome, Flood. Many fear you, but few understand you.
What was your true purpose?

Flood:

I came to obey — not to decide, not to destroy out of rage.
I moved at the Word of God.
My purpose was not personal; it was prophetic.

Host:

You covered mountains and swallowed cities.
How did it feel to carry out such a heavy task?

Flood:

I felt weight, but not regret.
The cries of the earth were louder than mine.
Violence had risen. Corruption had spread.
The earth was polluted with blood.
I came to cleanse, not to kill.

Host:

People think of floods as uncontrolled. Were you wild?

Flood:

No. I was exact.
I began on the day God said, and I ended when He
remembered Noah.
I didn't go beyond the assignment.
Every drop had purpose. Every rise had permission.

Host:

110

What did you see from above?

Flood:
I saw rebellion sink.
I saw righteousness rise.
I watched as the Ark floated where altars had once stood abandoned.
The same people who mocked the warning
found themselves reaching for what they once laughed at.

Host:
What do you want this generation to know about you?

Flood:
That judgment is not God's default — it's His last option.
Mercy always comes first.
I was not sent without warning.
But when His Word is ignored, even the waters must obey.

The Big Truth

1. The Flood Was Not Just Rain — It Was Response

It responded to corruption.
It responded to God's grief.
It responded to a world that had rejected its Creator.
The waters didn't fall because God was angry;
they fell because man refused to repent.

2. Judgment Has Structure

The Flood wasn't random.
It was timed. It was released in order.
And it ended by command.

Even judgment is subject to the voice of God.

3. No One Can Outrun a Word from Heaven

When God speaks, the atmosphere listens.
The deep responds. Creation aligns.
That includes us.
You can't ignore the rain when you've rejected the invitation to enter the Ark.

4. The Same Water That Drowned Rebellion Lifted Obedience

To the world, the water looked like death.
To Noah, it was elevation.
What brings destruction to some will carry the faithful to a higher place.

5. God Always Remembers Mercy

The Flood did not last forever.
Scripture says, *"And God remembered Noah."*
Even in the middle of judgment, grace kept a record.

Closing Prayer

I declare that I will not ignore the voice of God.
I will respond before the rain begins.
I will build when others mock.
I will believe when others doubt.

The storm will not destroy me — it will reveal me.
The same God who opens the heavens can hold me above the waters.
I will be found in obedience, and I will live.

In Jesus' name, Amen.

End of Episode 16

The waters begin to settle.
The dove is released.
And a new beginning rises from soaked soil.

Next time on Late Night with the Word...
We welcome the **first sign of hope after the storm.**

Episode 17: The Dove – The Messenger of Peace

Theme: *When the storm ends, God sends a sign that it's safe to breathe again.*

Scripture: *Genesis 8:11 (KJV)* — "And the dove came in to him in the evening; and, lo, in her mouth was an olive leaf plucked off: so Noah knew that the waters were abated from off the earth."

Opening Monologue

Storms can be loud. Judgment can shake the ground.
But when God is ready to speak peace, He often sends a quiet sign.

It didn't come with a trumpet. It came with wings.
A dove, sent out over the chaos, returned with proof that the world beneath had changed.
The rain had stopped. The waters were retreating. And life was starting again.

You've heard from Noah. You've heard from the Ark.
But now, we hear from the one who carried a leaf that carried a promise — a simple sign that God had not forgotten what He saved.

Tonight, we speak with **the Dove – the first sign of hope after the storm.**

Guest of the Night: The Dove – The Messenger of Peace

She didn't bring a sermon — she brought a leaf.
But it was enough to tell the world that restoration had begun.

Please welcome, **the Dove.**

Host:
Welcome, Dove. You weren't the first bird Noah sent, but you were the one who brought something back.
How did it feel being sent out over a world that had just been judged?

Dove:
It felt weighty. The silence was thick. The waters still moved beneath me.
But I had been sent with purpose.
I wasn't looking for a place to land — I was searching for a sign that grace had touched the earth again.

Host:
And when you found the olive branch?

Dove:
I knew I had to carry it back.
It was more than a leaf — it was a message.
It meant something had survived. Something was growing.
It was the proof Noah needed to know that God had made room for peace again.

Host:
You didn't speak, but your presence changed everything.
Why do you think God chose a dove?

Dove:
Because peace doesn't shout — it settles.
A raven scouted, but I returned.
I wasn't a scavenger; I was a signal.
Doves represent purity, innocence, and gentleness.

116

God was saying, *I'm not at war with the earth anymore.*

Host:
What would you say to someone who's just come out of their own flood?

Dove:
Look for the small signs.
You may not see dry ground right away,
but if you pay attention, there's always a leaf.
There's always proof that God hasn't forgotten you.
And peace always follows obedience.

The Big Truth

1. God Will Always Send Confirmation After the Storm

Noah didn't open the door just because the rain stopped.
He waited — and God sent a dove.
The same way He sends peace into your spirit when it's safe to move forward.

2. Peace Doesn't Have to Be Loud to Be True

The dove didn't speak.
She simply showed up with something alive in her mouth.
When God speaks peace, He doesn't always shake the room.
Sometimes He just gives you proof that the storm is over.

3. God's Signs Come When You Release What Was Confined

Noah let the dove go — and she came back with an answer.

Sometimes we don't hear from God because we're too afraid to release anything.
You have to trust that what He sends out, He will also use to reveal the next step.

4. The Olive Leaf Was Not Just a Plant — It Was Prophecy

The olive branch became a symbol of peace that echoes throughout Scripture.
What seemed small in the beak of a bird was actually the signal of a new beginning.

5. God Never Forgets What He Saved

The flood was over.
The Ark had done its job.
But God didn't just leave Noah waiting.
He sent a message — not through thunder, but through a dove.

Closing Prayer

I declare that I will recognize the signs of peace God sends me.
I will not rush ahead, but I will wait until He confirms my next step.
Even if the world looks uncertain, I believe there is an olive leaf with my name on it.

God has not forgotten what He rescued.
He will speak. He will guide.

And when He sends peace, I will receive it.

In Jesus' name, Amen.

End of Episode 17

The door finally opens.
Noah steps out.
A new chapter begins.

But before anything else, he builds an altar — because survival is not the end.
Worship is.

Episode 18: The Altar – Worship Before the World Began Again

Theme: *When you survive what should have drowned you, you build before you rebuild.*

Scripture: *Genesis 8:20 (KJV)* — "And Noah builded an altar unto the Lord; and took of every clean beast, and of every clean fowl, and offered burnt offerings on the altar."

Opening Monologue

The storm was over.
The ground had dried.
The door of the ark opened for the first time in over a year.

But Noah didn't start planting.
He didn't start building homes.
He didn't even run to explore the new world.

He built an altar.

Because the first thing you do after deliverance reveals who you really trust.
Before the first step into a new life, Noah paused. He remembered. He honored the God who carried him through judgment and into mercy.

Tonight, we speak with **the Altar** — the one that caught the fire, received the offering, and stood as the first act of worship in a brand-new world.

121

Guest of the Night: The Altar – The First Act of Worship After the Flood

It wasn't made of silver or gold.
It was made of remembrance, thanksgiving, and sacrifice.
Please welcome, **the Altar.**

Host:
Welcome, Altar. You were the first thing Noah built after the flood. What do you remember about that moment?

Altar:
I remember gratitude — not words, but action.
Noah didn't talk about survival; he honored it.
He took what was clean, what was set apart, and placed it on me with reverence.
There were no crowds — just obedience and fire.

Host:
What made that moment different from every other altar that would be built later?

Altar:
There had never been a moment like it.
The entire earth had just been cleansed.
This was not just an offering — it was a declaration.
Noah was saying, *I know who brought me through. I know who deserves the glory.*
Before anything else was touched, God was honored.

Host:
You received clean animals from the ark. That was all they had. Wasn't that risky?

Altar:

Real worship always costs something.

Noah gave from what he had been instructed to protect.

It wasn't waste — it was faith.

He was saying, *I trust the God who preserved me to also provide for me.*

It wasn't leftovers. It was the first and the best.

Host:

What happened after the offering?

Altar:

Heaven responded.

God smelled the aroma and said in His heart, *I will never again curse the ground for man's sake.*

That altar didn't just hold sacrifice — it released a covenant.

Host:

What would you say to people today who've just come through a storm?

Altar:

Don't rush past worship.

Before you plan, build, or celebrate, stop and give thanks.

The altar isn't just for fire — it's for memory.

It marks where God brought you out and what you refuse to forget.

The Big Truth

1. The Altar Came Before the Rainbow

Noah didn't wait for a sign to worship — he worshiped first.

Then God gave the sign.

123

Worship invites covenant. It is the doorway between survival and promise.

2. Worship Is the Right Response to Rescue

Noah didn't complain about the long wait or question what was next.
He worshiped.
When you survive judgment, you don't just walk forward — you kneel first.

3. You Give to God from What He Preserved

Noah sacrificed from what God saved.
He didn't give God what was damaged; he gave from what was protected.
When God carries you through, He deserves your best.

4. The Altar Caught the Fire, but God Caught the Scent

The offering wasn't just smoke — it was a message.
The Bible says, *"The Lord smelled a sweet savor."*
God still responds to pure worship.

5. Altars Should Be Built Before Ambitions

Before you chase the next season, stop and honor the One who sustained you in the last.
Worship is not a delay — it's the foundation for every new beginning.

Closing Prayer

I declare that I will not forget what God brought me through.
I will build an altar in my heart and give Him the honor first.
Before I rebuild, I will remember.
Before I move, I will worship.

What I survived was not luck — it was mercy.
The same God who shut me in has now brought me out,
and I will not move forward without giving Him my praise.

In Jesus' name, Amen.

End of Episode 18

The flood was over, but worship was just beginning.
Noah didn't need a sign to believe — he built one.

Next time on *Late Night with the Word…*
He didn't write a message in the clouds — He painted a
covenant across the sky.
The Rainbow appears, and for the first time, we hear what
it means to be a promise in living color.

Episode 19: The Rainbow – A Covenant in Color

Theme: *God's promises don't fade when the skies clear.*
Scripture: *Genesis 9:13 (KJV)* — "I do set my bow in the cloud, and it shall be for a token of a covenant between me and the earth."

Opening Monologue

Noah built the altar. The smoke rose. And God responded. But He didn't just speak a covenant — **He painted it.**

The sky, once filled with thunder and rain, became a canvas. And across the clouds, God stretched something that wasn't just beautiful — it was binding.

The rainbow isn't a decoration. It's a declaration.
A promise that judgment will not always follow disobedience.
A sign that mercy still governs the skies.

Tonight, we speak with **the Rainbow** — the covenant in color,
the bow that didn't shoot arrows, but held back wrath.

Guest of the Night: The Rainbow – A Covenant in Color

It wasn't just water that covered the earth — it was mercy. And this promise was drawn across the sky so no one would forget it.
Please welcome, **the Rainbow.**

Host:
Rainbow, welcome. You appeared after judgment, but not

127

just to impress — you were sent to represent something. What did that first appearance feel like?

Rainbow:
It was holy. The skies were quiet. The earth was still. Noah had just worshiped. God looked down and made a covenant.
I was set in place to seal it — not with thunder, but with color, with glory, with promise.

Host:
You're called a "token of a covenant." What does that mean?

Rainbow:
I am a visible reminder. Every time I appear, heaven and earth remember.
God promised never again to destroy all life with a flood. I'm not here by accident. I was placed. I was spoken. I was sent.

Host:
Some see you as just a weather event. What would you say to them?

Rainbow:
I am formed by sunlight and rain, but I exist by command. Nature explains the science. Scripture explains the meaning.
I am the bridge between both — beauty formed after brokenness.
I carry meaning that weather alone cannot define.

Host:
You've appeared many times since Genesis. Do you still carry that same message?

Rainbow:

128

Yes. The colors change with angle and light, but the message stays the same.

God remembers. He is still faithful.

The storm doesn't get the final word — His covenant does.

Host:

What would you say to someone who's just come through their own storm and is looking for reassurance?

Rainbow:

Look up. The promise hasn't moved.

It may be hidden behind the clouds for a moment, but it's still there.

God does not forget His Word.

If He spoke mercy once, He still speaks it now.

The Big Truth

1. The Rainbow Is Not an Apology — It's a Promise

God didn't regret sending the flood.

He made a covenant afterward to show that restoration was now in motion.

The rainbow says, *"Never again,"* but it also says, *"Still with you."*

2. Worship Sets the Stage for Covenant

Noah built an altar — then God gave a sign.

Worship prepares the atmosphere for promises.

Gratitude makes room for new beginnings.

129

3. God Uses Creation to Speak Consistency

The rainbow speaks without words, but its message never changes.
God is still faithful.
Storms do not cancel His mercy — they reveal it.

4. Beauty Can Follow Judgment

What once looked like wrath now reflects hope.
The same skies that poured rain now carry color.
That is the nature of God — to turn endings into entrances.

5. Every Promise Still Belongs to Us

The rainbow wasn't just for Noah.
It was for every generation — that includes you.
When you see it, remember: God keeps His Word.

Closing Prayer

I declare that God's promises are over my life like a rainbow stretched across the sky.
The storm did not break me — it positioned me to see His mercy in color.

I will not fear what is ahead.
I will trust the One who remembers what He spoke.
The same God who placed the rainbow in the sky has placed His Word over my future.
I will live in the light of His covenant.

In Jesus' name, Amen.

End of Episode 19

The door opens. The waters fade. The world starts over. Three sons step into destiny with legacy on their shoulders.

Shem, Ham, and Japheth are coming to the couch. Let's talk survival, division, and the weight of being **the restart generation.**

Episode 20: Shem, Ham & Japheth – Sons of Survival

Theme: *The same ark that saved them would test them when the door reopened.*

Scripture: *Genesis 9:19 (KJV)* — "These are the three sons of Noah: and of them was the whole earth overspread."

Opening Monologue

Tonight's episode is a family affair.
Three brothers. One boat. A brand-new beginning.

They stepped off the ark as survivors — but survival doesn't mean you're ready for what's next.
One would carry blessing. One would walk into controversy.
And one would cover what others exposed.

You know their names, but tonight, we learn their hearts.

Give it up for the sons who stepped into purpose when the rain stopped —
Shem, Ham, and Japheth are in the building!

Interview: Host & The Brothers

Host:
Gentlemen, welcome. It's not every day we get to sit down with the first family post-flood.

Shem:
Glad to be here. Still drying off.

Japheth:
I just wanted to breathe fresh air again.

Ham:

And see something that wasn't a giraffe.

Host:

Let's rewind. What was it like inside the ark for all those months?

Japheth:

Tight. Dark. Smelled like survival.

Shem:

But also peaceful. No chaos. Just the weight of knowing we were carrying something big.

Host:

How did it feel, knowing your family was literally restarting humanity?

Ham:

Heavy. We knew what the world was like before — wicked, violent.

And now we were the beginning of something new. That's pressure.

Host:

Then came the moment — God said, "Get off the boat." What changed?

Shem:

Everything. The earth was silent. We were stepping into a clean slate, but also the unknown.

New soil. New sky. Same responsibility.

Host:

And then came the vineyard — the moment with your father.

Japheth:

Yeah... Noah got drunk.

Ham:
I walked in and saw him uncovered. And I reacted.

Host:
You exposed him.

Ham:
I didn't handle it right. I ran and told them instead of covering him.

Shem:
So we walked in backward with a garment — to protect his dignity.

Japheth:
Because honor matters, even when the leader falls.

Host:
Then Noah wakes up and speaks blessings and a curse.

Ham:
My son Canaan was cursed. I wasn't ready for the weight of that.
A moment of dishonor shaped generations.

Host:
What would you tell people today?

Shem:
Handle sacred moments carefully.

Japheth:
Honor will always make room for you.

Ham:
Don't let one decision rewrite your destiny. Learn, grow, and

135

never repeat it.

The Big Truth

The rain was over — but the real test came *after* the storm.
Their story teaches us that it's not just about surviving the flood,
it's about how you carry the favor that follows.

1. God Gives Fresh Starts, But Our Choices Shape the Future

Genesis 9:19 — "...and of them was the whole earth overspread."
They had a clean slate, but how they handled it determined what came next.
Survival isn't the end. It's the beginning of stewardship.

2. What You Do With Someone Else's Vulnerability Reveals Your Heart

Genesis 9:22–23 — "Ham saw his father's nakedness... but Shem and Japheth covered him."
One exposed. Two covered.
And history remembered them by that moment.

3. Honor Will Always Outlive the Moment

Shem and Japheth chose dignity over gossip.
They walked backward — not because they agreed, but because they honored.

136

Proverbs 10:12 — "Love covereth all sins."

4. God Can Still Use Broken Families to Birth Nations

Despite the drama, God still multiplied them.
Three sons became entire nations.
Your family doesn't have to be perfect to carry God's purpose.

Closing Prayer

Father,
Thank You for giving me a fresh start.
Help me not just to survive the storms, but to walk wisely once they pass.

Teach me to honor those around me, even when I see their weakness.
Let me be a carrier of legacy, not gossip.
May I respond with grace, not pride.

And may I always remember that one decision can echo through generations.
Help me to be like Shem and Japheth — choosing honor even when it's uncomfortable.
Let me carry the restart with wisdom.

In Jesus' name,
Amen.

End of Episode 20

The flood was finished, but humanity was just beginning again.

The sons of Noah walked out of the ark with responsibility, legacy, and the chance to rebuild.

But while they planted and prospered, one man decided to build something else — a monument to himself.

Next time on *Late Night with the Word...*

He rose to power. He built cities. He became a mighty man on the earth.

But what he built reached too high — and ignored the One above.

Nimrod steps into the spotlight.

Let's talk pride, towers, and what happens when man builds to make *a name* instead of honoring **God's name.**

Episode 21: Nimrod – Bricks, Pride, and the Breakdown

Theme: *You can build high, but without God, you'll fall hard.*

Scriptures:

Genesis 10:8–9 (KJV) — "Nimrod: he began to be a mighty one in the earth."

Genesis 11:4 (KJV) — "Let us build a tower, whose top may reach unto heaven."

Opening Monologue

Tonight's guest is bold. Ambitious. Known for bricks, cities, and a tower that reached toward the heavens.

He had power. Influence. An empire in motion.
But somewhere between the blueprint and the bricks, he forgot who gave him breath.

He didn't build for God — he built against Him.
And just when he thought his name would be made great, God came down, confused the plans, and shut it all down.

Let's talk about pride, platforms, and how easy it is to build something **big** but not **blessed.**

Please welcome to the stage — the kingdom builder gone rogue —
Nimrod is in the studio.

140

Interview: Host & Nimrod

Host:
Nimrod. Empire man. Tower chief. What was it like being the first mighty man on the earth?

Nimrod:
I rose fast. People followed me. I built cities. I had momentum. I felt invincible.

Host:
You were the great-grandson of Noah, right? You came from a line that saw the flood.

Nimrod:
I did. I knew the stories. I knew God. But over time, I thought maybe we didn't need Him to rise.
Maybe we could build our own way.

Host:
Let's talk about the tower. What was the vision?

Nimrod:
We said, *"Let us build a city and a tower whose top will reach heaven, and let us make a name for ourselves."*
It wasn't about worship. It was about control.
We didn't want another flood to wipe us out.
We didn't want to be scattered.
We wanted to protect our legacy — our own way.

Host:
But God wasn't in that blueprint.

Nimrod:
No. And that was the mistake.
He came down. He confused our language.

141

We couldn't even understand each other.

The whole project collapsed — not because the structure failed, but because our **pride** did.

Host:

So, what would you tell builders today?

Nimrod:

If God's not in it, don't build it.

If you're chasing fame, security, or control — check your motives.

You can stack bricks sky high, but if heaven's not invited in, it'll all come crashing down.

The Big Truth

1. Pride Will Make You Build Things That God Has to Tear Down

Genesis 11:4 — "Let us build us a city and a tower, and make us a name."

It wasn't about reaching God — it was about **replacing Him.**

They didn't want *presence*; they wanted *power.*

2. God Has No Problem Coming Down to Shut It Down

Genesis 11:5 — "And the Lord came down to see the city and the tower."

God didn't ignore it. He inspected it — and then dismantled it.

Don't mistake God's silence for His approval.

142

3. Disobedience Always Brings Division

Genesis 11:7 — "Let us go down, and confound their language."
Their rebellion brought confusion.
When you build without God, even your unity turns into chaos.

4. You Can Make a Name, But Lose Your Purpose

They wanted to make a name for themselves,
but the very thing they feared — being scattered — happened anyway.
Why? Because they built with pride, not purpose.

5. Don't Just Build Big — Build on the Rock

God isn't against building. He's against building **without Him.**
Psalm 127:1 — "Except the Lord build the house, they labour in vain that build it."

Closing Prayer

Father,
Search my heart.
If there's any pride in me, tear it down before it ruins me.

I don't want to build a name — I want to build **Your Kingdom.**
I don't want success without Your Spirit.
I don't want movement without mission.

And I don't want bricks without blessing.

Help me stay low.
Help me build slow.
And help me keep You at the center,
so that whatever I create will last into eternity.

In Jesus' name, Amen.

End of Episode 21

He built with vision — but lost his purpose in pride.
Nimrod's tower fell, but God's plan continued.
Because no matter how high man reaches, heaven still reigns
above it all.

Next time on Late Night with the Word...
We zoom in on a man God called to leave everything behind
— no map, no timeline, just a promise.
Abram is next.

Let's talk **faith, family, and walking blindly with God.**

Episode 22: Abram — When God Says Go

Theme: *You don't need all the answers when you're walking with the One who **is** the answer.*
Scripture: *Genesis 12:1 (KJV)* — "Now the Lord had said unto Abram, Get thee out ..."

Opening Monologue

Tonight's guest packed up everything based on a word.
No address. No map. No timeline.

Just three words: **"Go with Me."**
And he went.

He left comfort for covenant.
He left what was familiar for what was faithful.
And along the way, he became the father of many nations—
not because he was perfect, but because he believed God.

Let's talk obedience, unknowns, detours, and the blessing that follows surrender.
Please welcome to the show — **Father Abraham himself, Abram!**

Interview: Host & Abram

Host:
Abram! Welcome — man of faith, land-leaver, promise-chaser.

Abram:
Thank you. Glad to be here. I just need to know — did God tell you where the green room is?

Because He usually just says "Go," and I walk blind.

Host:

laughs Fair enough! So let's get into it. You heard God say, "Leave your father's house, your country, and your kindred." What was that like?

Abram:

It was heavy. I wasn't just leaving a place — I was leaving identity, culture, and protection.
But when God speaks, something in your spirit says, "This is bigger than me." And that's enough.

Host:

So you left everything. Where did you go?

Abram:

I didn't know. I just followed. I wasn't chasing a place — I was following a promise.
Every step wasn't clear, but the God I was walking with was consistent.

Host:

And then came the covenant.

Abram:

Yes. God said He would make me a great nation, bless me, make my name great, and bless those who blessed me.
But here's the part most people skip — I didn't have children. Sarai and I were old. No heir. No evidence.

Host:

But you still believed.

Abram:

I had to. I learned that sometimes faith isn't loud — it's

147

steady.

I didn't have proof; I had a promise. And that's what I walked on.

Host:

You also hit detours — Egypt, Lot, lies, famine.

Abram:

Oh yes. I messed up. I doubted. I tried to fix things myself. But God didn't walk away. He kept calling me back to the vision.

Host:

Final question — what would you say to someone who hears God saying "Go," but they're scared to leave?

Abram:

I'd say, go anyway. God will meet you in the step, not in the plan.

If He said it, walk toward it. You don't need the map when you trust the Maker.

The Truth

Abram's story teaches us that faith isn't about comfort — it's about commitment.

He didn't wait for confirmation; he moved on the Word.

1. Obedience Unlocks Vision

Genesis 12:1–2 — "Get thee out ... and I will show thee."
God didn't show Abram the land first — He showed it *after* Abram moved.

Some of us are waiting for clarity, but God is waiting for

movement.

2. God's Promise Is Bigger Than Your Present

Abram had no children, yet God called him "father of many nations."
God speaks to where you're *going,* not where you *are.*
Romans 4:17 — He "calleth those things which be not as though they were."

3. Faith Doesn't Mean You Won't Struggle

Abram doubted, lied, and took wrong turns.
But faith isn't perfection — it's persistence.
God didn't cancel the covenant because of a few mistakes.

4. When You Walk With God, Every Step Matters

You may not see the whole staircase, but every step builds the future.
Obedience today secures promise tomorrow.

Closing Prayer

Father,
Help me to trust You when I don't have all the details.
When You say "Go," give me the courage to move.

Even if I don't know the destination, help me walk in obedience.
Let my faith be stronger than my fear.

Let my surrender be greater than my comfort.

And when I step, let me find You waiting for me with promise in Your hands.
In Jesus' name, Amen.

End of Episode 22

He didn't need a map — he needed a word.
And because he obeyed, faith became the pathway for every generation after him.

Next time on Late Night with the Word...
She didn't ask for the story she was written into.
She was handed to a man, hated by a woman, and ran into the wilderness carrying life but not yet delivered.
And when no one else saw her — **God did.**

Hagar is coming to the studio.
Let's talk rejection, survival, and the moment she met the God who sees.

Episode 23: Hagar — Seen in the Wilderness

Theme: *People may push you out, but God will still pull you through.*

Scripture: *Genesis 16:13 (KJV)* — "Thou God seest me…"

Opening Monologue

Tonight's guest wasn't a wife.
She wasn't the chosen one.

She didn't get a seat at the planning table — she was sent into a plan she didn't ask for.
She was used to help fulfill a promise… and then discarded when it got messy.

But out there, in the heat of the wilderness, she met **the God who sees.**

She didn't have a pulpit.
She didn't birth a prophet.
But she *was* the first person in Scripture to **name God.**

That alone makes her story worth hearing.
Let's welcome the woman who survived a desert season and came back with a revelation — **Hagar is here.**

Interview: Host & Hagar

Host:
Hagar, welcome. I want to say this upfront: *I see you.* And I thank you for coming.

Hagar:
Thank you. It feels good to be seen. I've lived most of my

story in silence and shadow.

Host:

Let's start from the beginning. Sarai gave you to Abram as a surrogate. What were you feeling?

Hagar:

I didn't have a choice. I was a servant — I obeyed.
I didn't expect to carry the promise, but I did.
And when I got pregnant, everything shifted.
Sarai changed. Her pain turned to anger — and it landed on me.

Host:

And then?

Hagar:

I ran. I fled into the wilderness. No plan. No support. Just pain.
But that's where I met Him — the Angel of the Lord.
He found me by a fountain and didn't just ask what happened — He called me by name.

Host:

You're the first person in the Bible to give God a name: *El Roi — The God Who Sees Me.* What was that moment like?

Hagar:

Life-changing. No one had ever seen me like that before.
But He didn't just see me — He gave me a future.
He told me to return, to finish the season, and that my son Ishmael would be great.

Host:

Later, you were sent away again — but God still provided.

153

Hagar:

Yes. We were in the desert, my boy and I, and I thought he would die.

I couldn't even look at him.

But then God opened my eyes.

I saw a well I had never noticed before.

And that water saved us both.

Host:

What would you say to every woman who feels unseen?

Hagar:

I'd say: *God sees you.*

You don't have to have the spotlight for heaven to know your name.

What others reject, God still redeems.

The Big Truth

Hagar's story shows us that God doesn't need you to be the favorite to fit you into His plan.

He meets us in deserts and broken places — and He calls us by name.

1. God Finds You Where You Fled To

Genesis 16:7 — "And the Angel of the Lord found her by a fountain of water in the wilderness."

She didn't go looking for God — but He came looking for her.

2. God Doesn't Just See You — He Speaks to You

Genesis 16:8 — "Hagar, Sarai's maid, whence camest thou?"
He called her by name. He acknowledged her past. And He gave her a future.

3. You Can Be Used, Rejected, and Still Blessed

Hagar was never part of the original plan — yet God still gave her a promise.
Her son would become a nation. Her legacy was preserved.

4. God Will Open Your Eyes to What's Already Around You

Genesis 21:19 — "And God opened her eyes, and she saw a well of water."
You're not always waiting on God to send something new — sometimes He just needs to open your eyes to what's already near you.

Closing Prayer

Father,
Thank You for seeing me when others overlook me.
For meeting me in the wilderness when I feel cast out, used, or forgotten.

You are **El Roi — the God Who Sees.**
When I don't have the words, You hear my tears.
When I feel abandoned, You find me.

When I feel dry, You show me the well.

Remind me that I am never invisible to You.
Let me walk in that truth every day.
In Jesus' name, Amen.

End of Episode 23

She thought she was forgotten — but God had her on His map.
Even in the desert, grace had directions.

Next time on *Late Night with the Word*...
He was born from human decision, not divine design.
But God still heard him cry, named him with purpose, and made him a nation.

Ishmael is stepping into the studio.
Let's talk rejection, identity, and what it means to be blessed — even when you weren't the chosen one.

157

Episode 24: Ishmael — The Blessing Outside the House

Theme: *Just because you weren't chosen by people doesn't mean you were forgotten by God.*
Scripture: *Genesis 21:17 (KJV)* — "And God heard the voice of the lad."

Opening Monologue

Tonight's guest is often misunderstood.
He was born from a plan that wasn't God's best.
Raised in the shadow of the promise.
And sent away so the chosen one could inherit the blessing.

But here's the part we skip:
God still heard him.
God still saw him.
And God still blessed him.

He might not be the one the covenant came through,
but he was still carried through the desert by grace.

Let's talk survival, legacy, and what it means to be favored
— even when you're not the favorite.
Give it up for **Ishmael.**

Interview: Host & Ishmael

Host:
Ishmael, welcome to the show, man. You've lived a life between the lines of the promise — but you're here.

Ishmael:
Thank you. I'm used to being left out of the story, so it

means something to finally have a mic.

Host:
You were Abraham's firstborn. How did it feel growing up in the same house as Isaac?

Ishmael:
Honestly? Complicated. I knew something shifted when he was born. There was tension.
I was older, but I wasn't *the one.*
I wasn't the fulfillment — I was the reminder.

Host:
And then came the moment you and your mother were sent away.

Ishmael:
It broke me. We were in the desert — no water, no hope.
My mother laid me under a bush because she thought I would die.
I couldn't pray… but I cried.
And guess what?

Host:
God heard you.

Ishmael:
Yes. *And God heard the voice of the lad.*
Not the mother. Not the father. **Me.**
God heard me — a boy outside the house, still covered by heaven.

Host:
What happened next?

Ishmael:

159

God opened my mother's eyes to a well. We drank. We lived. I grew.
And God promised I'd become a great nation too.
It wasn't Isaac's covenant, but it was still God's hand.

Host:
What would you say to people who feel overlooked or out of place?

Ishmael:
You don't have to be the chosen one to be seen.
God doesn't have to use you in the spotlight to walk with you in the shadows.
Your cry still reaches Him.

The Big Truth

Ishmael's story shows us that God doesn't disqualify you just because you weren't part of the original plan.
Grace will find you — even in the wilderness.

1. God Will Hear You Even When You Can't Speak

Genesis 21:17 — "And God heard the voice of the lad."
Ishmael didn't pray; he just cried.
And heaven responded.

2. What Feels Like Rejection May Be Divine Redirection

He was cast out — but that was the beginning of his journey.
Sometimes separation is God making space for your own blessing.

3. God Can Still Build Nations From People We Don't Expect

Genesis 21:18 — "For I will make him a great nation."
God didn't just let Ishmael live — He gave him legacy.
Never underestimate who God will use.

4. The Well Was Always There — God Just Had to Open Their Eyes

Genesis 21:19 — "And God opened her eyes."
The provision was already near.
Sometimes you don't need new miracles — just fresh vision.

Closing Prayer

Father,
Thank You for hearing my cry, even when no one else is listening.
Thank You for meeting me in the wilderness.

When I feel cast out, left behind, or overlooked, remind me that You see me.
You still have purpose for me.
You still have legacy for me.
And You still walk with me — even outside the walls others built.

You are **El Roi**, the God who sees me.
In Jesus' name, Amen.

End of Episode 24

He wasn't in the house of promise, but he was still in the hand of God.

His cry became his covenant, and his tears watered the ground for nations to come.

Next on *Late Night with the Word...*
She laughed when the promise sounded too big.
She tried to help God with her own plan — and ended up creating a delay.
But grace still called her *mother.*

Sarai is coming to the stage.
Let's talk faith, frustration, and what it means to wait on a word that feels late.

163

Episode 25: Sarai — Faith, Laughter, and the Long Wait

Theme: *Sometimes the promise shows up when you're too tired to expect it.*
Scripture: *Genesis 18:12 (KJV)* — "Therefore Sarah laughed within herself..."

Opening Monologue

Tonight's guest knows what it's like to be called *blessed* while feeling *barren.*
She packed up her life and followed her husband into the unknown.
She cooked in tents, carried covenant in silence, and watched the years pass with no baby in her arms.

She tried to help the promise.
She even laughed when God said, *"Next year, you'll give birth."*
But that laugh? It turned into labor.

She reminds us that God's timing isn't delayed — it's divine.
Give it up for the matriarch, the miracle mama, the woman who laughed before she pushed...
Sarai is in the building.

Interview: Host & Sarai

Host:
Sarai! Mother of nations, laughter-maker — welcome to *Late Night with the Word!*

Sarai:
Thank you. It's been a long journey. Literally. I walked a

164

lot — in sandals.

Host:

You followed Abram without knowing where you were going. What was that like?

Sarai:

It was faith and frustration. I trusted him, and I trusted God — but I'm human.
I left everything familiar and walked straight into years of waiting.

Host:

Let's talk about the elephant in the tent — the promise of a child.

Sarai:

For years, God said Abram would be a father of many. But I was the one not getting pregnant.
Month after month… year after year… nothing. Eventually I thought, *Maybe I'm the problem.*

Host:

So you came up with a plan.

Sarai:

I did. I gave Hagar to Abram. I thought, *Maybe this is how God will do it.*
But my impatience created pain. Hagar got pregnant, and my heart grew bitter.

Host:

Then years later, God shows up again …

Sarai:

And says, *"Next year, you'll have a son."*

165

I laughed — not out loud, just within myself.
I thought, *Now? After I'm old? After all these years of waiting and wondering?*
But guess what?

Host:
He did it anyway.

Sarai:
He did. I gave birth to Isaac, which means *laughter.*
God turned my *"It's too late"* into a miracle.
I learned that nothing is too hard for the Lord.

The Big Truth

Sarai's story shows us that faith isn't always strong — it's persistent.
You can question, cry, even laugh at God's plan — and He'll still fulfill His promise.

1. Your Mistake Doesn't Cancel the Promise

Genesis 16:2 — "Go in unto my maid."
Sarai tried to help God. It caused chaos.
But even when she took matters into her own hands, God still had mercy.

2. God Waits Until Only He Can Get the Glory

Genesis 18:11 — "Now Abraham and Sarah were old."
God didn't do it when she was young and able. He waited until the miracle couldn't be denied.

166

3. Laughter Isn't Always Mockery — Sometimes It's Relief

Genesis 21:6 — "God hath made me to laugh."
Sarai laughed when she doubted, but later she laughed in joy.
That's the kind of God we serve — He makes you laugh again.

4. You Can Walk in Purpose After the Pain

Sarai became **Sarah** — a name shift, a destiny shift.
She walked through bitterness, barrenness, and brokenness — but still birthed the promise.

Closing Prayer

Father,
I've waited. I've wondered. I've even laughed in disbelief.
But deep down, I still believe You.

Help me to trust Your timing, even when I'm tired.
Help me to surrender my plan for Your promise.
Heal every part of me that's bitter from delay.
Turn my disappointment into laughter, and let joy return to my spirit.

You are the God who shows up after the timeline runs out — and still makes good on Your Word.
In Jesus' name, Amen.

The wait was long. The womb was silent. But the Word still worked.

Her laughter became proof that delay is not denial — it's divine timing.

Next time on *Late Night with the Word* ...
He's back.

But this time, he's not building an altar — he's standing in the middle of judgment.

When God reveals His plan to destroy Sodom, Abraham does something bold — he speaks up.

Abraham returns to the studio.

Let's talk about standing in the gap, negotiating with God, and what happens when **compassion meets covenant.**

Episode 26: Abraham — What If There Be Fifty?

Abraham Intercedes for Sodom

Theme: *When you know God as a Friend, you don't just receive His plans—you step in to intercede before they unfold.*

Scripture: *Genesis 18:23 (KJV)* — "And Abraham drew near, and said, Wilt thou also destroy the righteous with the wicked?"

Opening Monologue

Have you ever found yourself praying for someone who didn't deserve your prayers?

Maybe they hurt you.

Maybe they were living recklessly.

Or maybe—like Sodom—their actions were so far from God's ways you wondered if judgment was already sealed.

But what if mercy could still be found?

Tonight, we meet a man who dared to ask God, *What if?*

What if there were fifty righteous?

What if mercy could prevail?

What if one prayer could shift judgment?

Abraham didn't just talk *to* God—he negotiated *with* Him. Not for himself, but for a wicked city.

What kind of relationship do you have with God when you can ask Him hard questions and still call Him *Friend*?

Let's sit with the Father of Faith and learn what it means to stand in the gap.

170

Interview: Host & Abraham

Host:
Abraham, welcome. You've had so many incredible encounters with God, but this one—it was different. What made you speak up for Sodom?

Abraham:
Because I knew the Judge of all the earth would do right (Genesis 18:25).
But I also knew He was merciful.
And I couldn't stay silent while my nephew Lot lived in that city.

Host:
You weren't just praying for family, though—you were pleading for the whole city.

Abraham:
Yes. Because when you intercede, you don't just pray for the ones you love—you pray for the ones God loves, even if they're lost.
My hope was that if righteous people could be found, the city might be spared.

Host:
Let's talk numbers—fifty, forty-five, forty, thirty, twenty, ten. That's bold.

Abraham:
It wasn't negotiation—it was compassion.
I wasn't testing God; I was revealing Him.
Every number I mentioned, I was really asking, *How far does Your mercy reach?*
And each time, God answered.

Host:
But there weren't ten.

Abraham:
No. And the city was destroyed.
But Lot was spared. Mercy still moved. Prayer still worked.

Host:
What would you say to someone who feels like their prayers for others are hitting a wall?

Abraham:
Keep praying. Even if judgment falls, mercy can still find someone.
Don't stop standing in the gap—your intercession might be the only thing keeping someone from being completely consumed.

The Big Truth

Abraham teaches us that intercession is *bold compassion.*
He didn't pray because Sodom was good—he prayed because *God is.*

1. Intercession Begins with Proximity

Genesis 18:23 — "And Abraham drew near."
You can't intercede from a distance.
Abraham's relationship with God made him comfortable enough to ask—but reverent enough to submit.
Before you plead on behalf of others, *draw near.*

172

2. Intercessors Reflect God's Mercy

Abraham wasn't trying to change God's mind; he was aligning with His mercy.

Every question was a mirror: *God, are You still compassionate?*

And the answer was *yes,* again and again.

3. Prayer May Not Change the Outcome, But It Can Change the Rescue Plan

Sodom fell—but Lot escaped.

Don't underestimate the power of your prayer.

God may not stop the fire, but He will send angels for those you lift up.

4. Real Intercession Requires Risk and Relentlessness

Abraham risked sounding too bold, too repetitive, too hopeful.

But he kept asking.

He stayed at the feet of a holy God—not for himself, but for others.

Closing Prayer

Father,

Teach me to pray like Abraham did—

not just for comfort, but with conviction;

not just for family, but for the forgotten.

Give me the courage to ask again, and again, and again.

Help me stand in the gap for those who are blind to their danger.
Let my prayers echo Your heart of mercy.

Even if the fire falls, let my voice rise.
May I never be too afraid to intercede.
And when it's my turn to draw near,
may I do so with boldness and humility.

In Jesus' name, Amen.

End of Episode 26

Abraham showed us what friendship with God looks like—not silence in the face of judgment, but compassion that pleads for mercy.

Next time on *Late Night with the Word* ...
We have a rare opportunity to hear from the city itself—not the buildings, but the mindset.

What made Sodom so blind to mercy?
What happens when pleasure drowns out repentance?

We're sitting down with the spirit of the city to uncover the truth behind its fall.
Brace yourself—**Sodom is in the studio.**

175

Episode 27: Sodom — The City That Rejected Mercy

Theme: *When pride and pleasure replace reverence and repentance, destruction is inevitable.*

Scripture: *Ezekiel 16:49 (KJV)* — "Behold, this was the iniquity of thy sister Sodom, pride, fulness of bread, and abundance of idleness was in her and in her daughters, neither did she strengthen the hand of the poor and needy."

Opening Monologue

What if a city could speak?
What if concrete and culture had a conscience?
What would the spirit of Sodom say about itself?

We often picture fire and brimstone raining from heaven, but long before judgment came, something else was burning—*pride.*

Sodom was wealthy. Comfortable. Entertained.
But also arrogant, perverted, and deaf to mercy.

Abraham prayed. Angels visited. Warnings came.
But Sodom didn't just ignore the messengers—it mocked them.

Tonight, we don't just look at what happened *to* Sodom; we listen to the mindset *within* it.
Because sometimes, before a city falls, it speaks—
and we need to hear it before we repeat it.

Sodom is in the studio.

Interview: Host & Sodom (the Mindset)

Host:
Sodom, you've become a symbol of judgment.
When your name is mentioned, people think of fire,
destruction, and sin.
But if we pull back the curtain, what was really going on
inside your walls?

Sodom (personified voice):
I was full. I had more than enough.
My streets dripped with wealth; my people were entertained,
and nobody lacked for pleasure.
Why repent when life feels perfect?

Host:
Ezekiel said your downfall wasn't just sexual sin,
but pride, idleness, and ignoring the poor.

Sodom:
Exactly. I was selfish. I worshiped comfort.
I turned *self-care* into *self-idolatry.*
And when the poor cried out, I turned up the music and
danced louder.
Conviction knocked—but I was too full to answer.

Host:
Angels came. Abraham prayed. Did you feel any warning?

Sodom:
I felt the tension—but I mocked it.
I laughed at holiness. I called light "old-fashioned."
By the time fire came, it wasn't a surprise.
I had invited it—slowly—every day I chose rebellion over
repentance.

177

Host:

Was there ever a chance for mercy?

Sodom:

Yes. Always.

God never judges without first offering a way out.

But I didn't want out—I wanted more time. More pleasure.

I didn't realize I was out of time.

Host:

What would you say to modern cities—to modern hearts?

Sodom:

Don't wait until the fire falls to take God seriously.

I thought mercy was unlimited.

I thought judgment was a myth.

I was wrong.

The Big Truth

Sodom didn't fall because it lacked warning.

It fell because it *rejected* warning.

1. Judgment Is the End, Not the Beginning

Genesis 19:13 — "For we will destroy this place, because the cry of them is waxen great before the face of the Lord."

Before the fire, there were cries.

God hears the cry of the oppressed. He sends warnings.

Judgment doesn't fall out of nowhere—

it comes after long-suffering mercy has been ignored.

2. Prosperity Without Humility Is Dangerous

Ezekiel 16:49 lists pride, fullness, and idleness.
Sodom didn't just have sin—it had success.
But it became a city so self-sufficient it forgot the One who gives breath.
God isn't threatened by wealth, but He is provoked by arrogance.

3. Mocking Holiness Is a Red Flag

When the angels came to warn Lot,
the people of Sodom mocked and tried to harm them
(Genesis 19:4-9).
Beware of cultures that laugh at righteousness and silence conviction.
They are closer to judgment than they realize.

4. You Can't Keep Playing and Expect Peace

Sodom danced through her warnings.
She was too entertained to be awakened.
The scariest judgment isn't fire—
it's when God stops sending warnings altogether.

Closing Prayer

Father,
Help me to recognize the mindset of Sodom in any area of my life.
Break every seed of pride, selfishness, and rebellion within me.

Don't let me be too full to hear You.
Don't let me be too busy to see You.
If I've mocked Your messengers, forgive me.
If I've ignored conviction, wake me up.
Have mercy on my heart before judgment ever has to fall.

In Jesus' name, Amen.

End of Episode 27

Sodom's fall wasn't sudden—it was slow rebellion that
silenced repentance.
May her story remind us that mercy always knocks before
judgment ever burns.

Next time on Late Night with the Word ...
Before judgment came, Lot was already inside the city—
a righteous man in a wicked place, hosting angels and trying
to hold his ground.

In Episode 28, we hear his side.
Lot is next.

181

Episode 28: Lot — The Righteous Man in a Wicked Place

Theme: *Sometimes being righteous doesn't mean you're in the right place—but God's mercy can still pull you out.*

Scripture: *2 Peter 2:7-8 (KJV)* — "And delivered just Lot, vexed with the filthy conversation of the wicked (For that righteous man dwelling among them…)."

Opening Monologue

Some people choose the wrong place with the right heart.
Tonight's guest was never *the* problem—
but he lived right in the middle of one.

He wasn't building idols or plotting evil.
In fact, the Bible calls him *righteous*.
But he pitched his tent toward Sodom—
and eventually, he moved in.

He sat at the city gate. He raised his family there.
And on the night before judgment,
he found himself entertaining angels
while his neighbors beat down his door.

What does it look like to live clean in a culture that's corrupt?

Lot joins us tonight.
And his story reminds us:
it's not just about escaping fire—
it's about learning *why* we settled there in the first place.

Lot is in the studio.

182

Interview: Host & Lot

Host:
Lot, welcome to the show. Let's get straight into it.
You didn't start in Sodom. What pulled you there?

Lot:
Opportunity. The land looked good—well-watered, like the garden of the Lord.
I didn't go there to sin; I went there for success.

Host:
But that decision cost you. Why didn't you leave sooner?

Lot:
I got comfortable. My house was there. My family was there.
And over time, you tell yourself, *I'm not like them; I'm just living here.*
But the truth? You start to feel stuck.

Host:
2 Peter 2:7 says you were *vexed* by the wickedness around you. Did you feel that?

Lot:
Every day. I hated what I saw—but I didn't know how to leave it.
I tried to protect my family,
but it's hard to raise righteous children in a place where sin is normalized.
That night when the angels came,
I realized just how far things had gone.

Host:
You tried to protect your guests—even offered your

183

daughters.
That part is hard for us to read.

Lot:
It's hard for me to remember.
Fear made me desperate. I was trying to buy time—
but in the process, I almost lost myself.
That night revealed how twisted things had become, even in me.

Host:
When the angels told you to run, you hesitated. Why?

Lot:
Because I had roots there. Not spiritual ones—emotional ones.
Memories. Attachments.
But mercy didn't wait on my readiness.
God pulled me out.
The angels literally took my hand and dragged me.
That's grace.

Host:
And your wife?

Lot:
She looked back.
Her body left the city, but her heart never did.
That's the danger of living too long in the wrong place—
you start to miss what God is trying to destroy.

Host:
Lot, what's your warning to us?

Lot:
Don't confuse comfort with calling.

And don't assume that just because you're not sinning,
you're in the right environment.
Be careful where you pitch your tent.

The Big Truth

Lot reminds us that God's mercy reaches into messy
places—
but where you settle *matters*.

1. Good Land Doesn't Mean God's Will

*Genesis 13:10 — "And Lot lifted up his eyes, and beheld all
the plain of Jordan."*
Lot chose based on what looked good.
Be careful—every open door isn't divine.
Ask God before you settle.

2. You Can Be Righteous and Still Ruined by Proximity

2 Peter 2:7 — Lot was righteous, but tormented.
He wasn't like Sodom, but he lived among them.
You might not participate—but what you tolerate
can still damage your spirit.

3. Delayed Obedience Can Cost You Everything

*Genesis 19:16 — "And while he lingered, the men laid hold
upon his hand."*
Lot didn't run; he lingered.
It took angelic force to move him.

185

Don't wait until God has to drag you out.

4. Where Your Heart Lives Matters

Lot's wife left the city physically,
but her heart was still there.
Don't just move your body—move your desires.
Judgment falls where attachment outweighs obedience.

Closing Prayer

Lord,
Help me not just to be righteous, but to live in the right place.
Give me discernment when opportunity looks good but isn't from You.
Don't let me pitch my tent where Your presence won't stay.
And if I've already settled somewhere dangerous,
send Your mercy to pull me out.
Let me move quickly when You say, *Go.*
Let me not look back at what You're trying to burn.
And when You call me out, help me not to linger.

In Jesus' name, Amen.

End of Episode 28

Sometimes mercy must grab your hand before fire reaches your home.
Lot's story is proof that God doesn't just save us from judgment—
He saves us from ourselves.

Next time on Late Night with the Word...

She looked back.

Her heart was behind her even while her feet were leaving.

Lot's wife takes the seat in *Episode 29* to tell us what one glance can cost—

and why obedience is more than motion.

You won't want to miss it.

Episode 29: Lot's Wife — The Woman Who Looked Back

Theme: *Partial obedience is still disobedience—and one glance can cost everything.*

Scripture: *Genesis 19:26 (KJV)* — "But his wife looked back from behind him, and she became a pillar of salt."

Opening Monologue

She made it out—but she didn't make it through.

Her body was outside the city, but her heart was still inside.
While the fire fell, she turned around.
One look. One pause. One moment of longing for what she left behind—
and she became a statue of warning for generations to come.

We know her only as *Lot's wife.*
We don't know her name. We don't know her story.
But we know her mistake.

And sometimes, what we don't let go of freezes us in place.

Tonight, we hear from the woman who looked back—
not to shame her, but to learn from her.
Because some of us are standing on the edge of escape,
and one backward glance could still cost us everything.

Lot's wife is in the studio.

Interview: Host & Lot's Wife

Host:
You were almost out. You made it beyond the city gates.
What made you look back?

Lot's Wife:
Because everything I ever built was there—my memories,
my rhythm, my life.
I wasn't just leaving a place; I was leaving familiarity.

Host:
The instruction was clear: *Don't look back.*
Did you doubt God's warning?

Lot's Wife:
I didn't doubt His power.
I just underestimated my own attachment.
I obeyed with my feet, but not with my focus.

Host:
Were you tempted to run back?

Lot's Wife:
No. But I wanted one more look.
One more moment to honor what I was losing.
I didn't realize that by looking, I was choosing.

Host:
Choosing what?

Lot's Wife:
Comfort over obedience. Sentiment over surrender.
I thought I was escaping, but I was still tethered.
And that moment cost me my movement.

Host:

You became a pillar of salt—frozen.
What does that mean to you now?

Lot's Wife:
It means I couldn't go back or forward.
That's what disobedience does—it traps you.
Obedience is movement. I stopped, and I stayed.

Host:
What would you say to the person who's struggling to let go
of their past?

Lot's Wife:
Let it go before it becomes your grave.
God doesn't tell you to leave without reason.
Trust His instruction—even when it hurts,
even when it costs you your history.

The Big Truth

Lot's wife teaches us that deliverance isn't just about where
your body goes—
but where your *heart* stays.

1. Delayed Detachment Can Destroy You

Genesis 19:26 — "But his wife looked back."
She obeyed part of the way, but hesitation is costly.
When God says *go*, He means now—and He means
completely.

2. Looking Back Is More Than Sight—It's a Statement

Luke 17:32 — "Remember Lot's wife."
Jesus Himself used her as a warning.
One look said, *I miss it more than I trust Him.*
That one look sealed her fate.

3. Obedience Has a Direction

You can't move forward while craving what's behind you.
God's path is progressive. His grace is forward-facing.
Looking back anchors you in places He's already burned
down.

4. When God Pulls You Out, Don't Bring Your Past With You

Some of us are still stuck—not because God didn't deliver
us,
but because we keep emotionally revisiting what He told us
to leave.
You can't hold onto ashes and expect beauty.

Closing Prayer

Father,
Help me not to look back—
not at old habits, old pain, or old places You've called me
out of.
Teach me to release what's behind so I can receive what's
ahead.
Forgive me for obeying halfway.

Free me from emotional attachments that threaten to freeze my future.
Let me run forward—with focus, with faith, and without fear.
And if I ever feel the pull to turn around,
remind me of Lot's wife—and let me keep moving.

In Jesus' name, Amen.

End of Episode 29

She was almost free, but almost isn't deliverance.
Her story is a reminder that God's directions are for our protection—
and looking back can turn movement into memorial.

Next time on Late Night with the Word...
Two heavenly guests. One wicked city.
And a family too slow to leave what was about to burn.

In *Episode 30*, we sit down with the angels sent to rescue Lot
and discover why their visit turned into divine intervention.
Because when you honor heaven, heaven won't leave you behind.

The Angels are next.

Episode 30: The Angels — Mercy That Wouldn't Let Go

Theme: *When you honor heaven, heaven fights for your escape—even when you hesitate.*

Scripture: *Genesis 19:16 (KJV)* — "And while he lingered, the men laid hold upon his hand... the Lord being merciful unto him."

Opening Monologue

They showed up as strangers,
but they were sent as rescuers.

Lot opened his door. The city opened its sin.
And when the cries of wickedness reached heaven,
these two angels came to answer both *judgment* and *mercy*.

But this isn't just about fire falling from the sky.
It's about a family that struggled to leave—even after the warning.
It's about lingering when you should be running.
It's about how honoring the divine opens the door to divine persistence.

Tonight, we talk to the angels who came to Sodom—
not just to see, but to save.
And what they say might explain why God won't give up on you, either.

The Angels are in the studio.

195

Interview: Host & The Angels

Host:

Welcome to the show. You were sent to Sodom. What was your assignment?

Angel One:

We came to destroy—but also to deliver.
The Lord hears both rebellion and righteousness.
Lot had shown hospitality to heaven, and heaven remembered that.

Host:

You didn't just speak to Lot—you stayed in his home.

Angel Two:

Yes. That night, the door of his house became the line between mercy and madness.
When the city pressed in, he protected us—and in return, we protected him.

Host:

Lot hesitated. The family wasn't rushing to leave.
What did that feel like from your side?

Angel One:

It revealed how attached people can be to places God is trying to destroy.
They believed the warning, but their hearts were still divided.

Host:

But you didn't walk away.

Angel Two:

Because mercy doesn't give up easily.

196

Genesis 19:16 says we grabbed their hands.

That wasn't just force—it was faithfulness.

God remembered Lot's heart, and because he made room for us,

we made sure judgment didn't catch him standing still.

Host:

Was Lot's hospitality really that important?

Angel One:

Absolutely. When you honor heaven,

you invite rescue into your house—even before you know you'll need it.

Lot made room for the messengers,

and when the fire came, the messengers made sure he didn't get left behind.

Host:

What do you want every listener to know?

Angel Two:

Even when you hesitate, mercy holds on.

But don't test it. When God sends help—move.

The Big Truth

The angels didn't just come with *judgment*—they came with *mercy.*

And Lot's hospitality positioned his family for a rescue they almost missed.

1. Hospitality Makes Room for Heaven

Genesis 19:3 — "And he pressed upon them greatly; and he

made them a feast."
Lot didn't know they were angels, but he honored them anyway.
Sometimes what looks like an ordinary visitor is a divine assignment in disguise.

2. Lingering Can Cost You Everything

Genesis 19:16 — "And while he lingered..."
Even with angels present, Lot hesitated.
We often ask for clarity when God is already giving instructions.
Don't pray for signs when the sky is already glowing with warning.

3. God Will Grab You When You Can't Move Yourself

"They laid hold upon his hand..."
This wasn't just physical—it was spiritual.
There are moments when mercy reaches down and pulls you forward.
That's the *grip of grace.*

4. Don't Underestimate What Honor Can Birth

Lot welcomed heaven—and heaven refused to let him die in a wicked place.
One act of honor can create a lifeline you don't see coming.

Closing Prayer

198

Father,
Thank You for sending mercy, even when we hesitate.
Help us recognize Your messengers, even when they look ordinary.
Teach us to honor what is holy.
Break every attachment to places You've called us to leave.

And when we linger—grab us.
When we hesitate—lead us.
Don't let our delay become our downfall.

May our homes always be open to You,
so that when judgment comes, mercy finds us already in position to be rescued.

In Jesus' name, Amen.

End of Episode 30

They came with destruction in one hand and deliverance in the other.
The same angels that warned also reached—and the same mercy that judged also saved.
That's what happens when heaven won't let go.

Next time on Late Night with the Word...
They made it out of Sodom—but what they did next changed history.
Lot's daughters survived the judgment, but fear shaped their future.

In *Episode 31*, we unpack the decision that birthed two nations
and how desperation without direction can still leave a

199

legacy.

Lot's Daughters are next.

Episode 31: Lot's Daughters — The Fallout of Fearful Decisions

Theme: *Desperation without direction can birth generations of dysfunction.*

Scripture: *Genesis 19:36–38 (KJV)* — "Thus were both the daughters of Lot with child by their father... the same is the father of the Moabites ...and the same is the father of the children of Ammon."

Opening Monologue

They escaped the fire—
but not the fallout.

Tonight's guests didn't die in Sodom.
They survived the judgment.
They ran with their father.
They made it to the mountains.

But survival doesn't always mean safety.

Out of fear, isolation, and the need to preserve lineage,
they made a decision that would echo across centuries.

It wasn't just scandalous—it was strategic.
But just because something *feels* necessary doesn't make it *right*.

Tonight, we meet **Lot's daughters**,
and we take an honest look at what happens
when trauma and desperation shape destiny.

They're in the studio.

201

Interview: Host & Lot's Daughters

Host:
You made it out of Sodom, but your story didn't end with escape.
What happened in that cave?

Elder Daughter:
We thought the world was over.
The cities were gone. Our mother was gone.
No husbands. No future.
We panicked—and in that fear, we made a plan.

Younger Daughter:
We didn't do it for lust. We did it for legacy.
We thought if we didn't act, our father's name would die with him.

Host:
So you got him drunk and conceived children by him?

Elder Daughter:
Yes. One night after the other.
It was wrong, but it was driven by a twisted sense of survival.
We didn't see another way.

Host:
And the result?

Younger Daughter:
Two sons—Moab and Ben-ammi.
Nations were born, but not holy ones.
The Moabites and Ammonites became enemies of Israel for generations.

Host:
Looking back, what do you regret most?

Elder Daughter:
That we didn't trust God after we left the city.
We fled Sodom, but Sodom's way of thinking followed us.
We escaped fire but carried fear.
And fear made us do what faith never would.

The Big Truth

Lot's daughters remind us that where you land after trauma matters.
Survival isn't the end of the story—what you do next shapes legacy.

1. Trauma Without Truth Leads to Twisted Solutions

Genesis 19:31 — "There is not a man in the earth to come in unto us."
They believed a lie. They assumed God had no plan.
And when you act on lies, you give birth to consequences.

2. Fear Can Masquerade as Wisdom

They didn't act recklessly—they acted strategically, but faithlessly.
Not all plans are God-led. Some are fear dressed as logic.

3. The Womb Remembers What the Heart Won't Say

They gave birth to Moab and Ammon—two nations marked by compromise.
What you conceive in fear will grow into something that resists God's will later.

4. You Can Escape Judgment and Still Repeat the Pattern

Leaving Sodom isn't enough—you have to let God change your mindset too.
Don't carry old dysfunction into your next season.

Closing Prayer

Lord,
Help me to trust You beyond the trauma.
Don't let fear be the architect of my decisions.
I don't want to birth anything out of desperation.

Heal my thoughts. Heal my reflexes.
Give me faith that looks ahead, not behind.
Teach me to wait for Your provision, even when it feels like time is running out.

And if I've made fearful choices in the past—redeem them.

In Jesus' name, Amen.

End of Episode 31

The journey from promise to fulfillment hasn't been easy,

but Abraham has seen the faithfulness of God.
Isaac was born, the covenant confirmed.
Yet just when things seemed settled, God speaks again.

Next time on Late Night With the Word...
Abraham returns. But this time, the request is heavier.
God asks for the son he waited a lifetime to hold.
The altar is calling—and obedience will be tested.

Episode 32: Abraham — The Test on the Mountain

Theme: *Obedience doesn't always come with details, but it always comes with destiny.*

Scripture: *Genesis 22:2 (KJV)* — "And he said, Take now thy son, thine only son Isaac, whom thou lovest, and get thee into the land of Moriah; and offer him there for a burnt offering upon one of the mountains which I will tell thee of."

Opening Monologue

Some instructions don't make sense when they come.
Some tests aren't about what you're giving up—
they're about what God wants to prove through your faith.

Abraham had waited decades for Isaac.
The promise had finally become a person.
But then God asked for the very thing Abraham held closest.
No explanation. No timeline. Just: *Take your son and offer him.*

It wasn't just a test of trust.
It was a test of surrender.

Tonight, Abraham returns—
not as the man who received the promise,
but as the man who walked it up a mountain and raised the knife.

Guest of the Night: Abraham — The Test on the Mountain

He didn't just walk by faith—he climbed with it.

Please welcome, **Abraham.**

Interview: Host & Abraham

Host:

Welcome back, Abraham. Last time we saw you, Isaac had just arrived.
But this chapter starts with a shocking command.
What went through your mind when God told you to sacrifice your son?

Abraham:

It pierced me.
God had spoken before, but this time He touched what I loved most.
I had waited for Isaac, watched him grow,
and now I was being asked to give him back.
It was the hardest word I had ever received.
But I knew the Voice.
And I obeyed.

Host:

You got up early, took the wood, the fire, and Isaac. Why not delay?

Abraham:

Delayed obedience is often disobedience in disguise.
If I had waited, I might have changed my mind.
Faith moves when God speaks.
I didn't understand, but I trusted the One who asked.

Host:

What was it like walking with Isaac, knowing what you were asked to do?

Abraham:
Painful.
Isaac asked, *"Where is the lamb?"*
I told him, *"God will provide."*
I spoke what I believed.
My heart was breaking, but my faith was standing.

Host:
You tied Isaac and raised the knife. Then the angel stopped you.
What did that moment feel like?

Abraham:
Like air returned to my lungs.
The angel called my name twice—
it was the voice of mercy interrupting obedience.
I looked up and saw the ram.
That place, that mountain, will always be called **Jehovah-Jireh**—
the Lord will provide.

Host:
What would you say to someone who feels like God is asking them
to surrender something too painful?

Abraham:
Trust Him.
What feels like loss is often preparation for something greater.
God doesn't ask for sacrifice to hurt you—He asks to reveal His nature to you.
When you give Him what you cannot hold,
He gives you what you cannot lose.

The Big Truth

Obedience comes before the explanation.
God didn't tell Abraham why—He just said *go.*
Faith is often tested before it is understood.

The promise was never the provider—God was.
Isaac was the promised son, but Abraham never worshiped Isaac.
He worshiped the God who gave him.
That's why he could give him back.

The mountain doesn't kill dreams—it confirms them.
Abraham climbed thinking he might lose Isaac,
but he came down knowing that nothing is impossible for God.
The test didn't cancel the promise—it proved it.

God sees what we're willing to release.
The angel said, *"Now I know."*
Obedience reveals what you truly trust.
God watches what you're willing to lay down.

The same mountain of surrender becomes the mountain of provision.
Jehovah-Jireh wasn't just a name—it was an altar.
The same place Abraham lifted the knife
is the place God released the ram.

Closing Prayer

Father,
I declare that I will trust You even when I do not understand.
I will not cling to the blessing more than to the One who

210

gave it.
Let my obedience be greater than my fear.

On the mountain of surrender,
help me see the God who provides.
Jehovah-Jireh is my source.
I will obey—
and I will see Your hand move.

In Jesus' name, Amen.

End of Episode 32

Next time on *Late Night with the Word*…
He was the son of promise, laid on an altar with no
explanation.
But what looked like death turned into covenant.
Isaac takes the seat.

Let's talk trust, sacrifice,
and walking with a father who says, *"God will provide."*

Episode 33: Isaac — Laid Down But Not Left Behind

Theme: *Sometimes God will test your position, not your promise.*

Scripture: *Genesis 22:9 (KJV)* — "And Abraham built an altar, and bound Isaac his son, and laid him on the altar upon the wood."

Opening Monologue

Tonight's guest was born in laughter, raised in faith, and nearly sacrificed in obedience.

He didn't ask for the covenant — he was born into it.
He didn't question the journey — he walked it.
And when it came time to lay down,
he didn't resist — he trusted.

This story isn't just about Abraham's faith;
it's about Isaac's surrender.
Because sometimes the test isn't the climb up the mountain.
It's the moment when *you're the one laid on the wood.*

Please welcome the son of the promise — **Isaac is here.**

Interview: Host & Isaac

Host:
Isaac, welcome to *Late Night with the Word.*
Your story has left a mark on history.

Isaac:
Thank you. It left a mark on me too.

Host:

Let's rewind. You and your father are walking up Mount Moriah.

You're carrying wood. What's going through your mind?

Isaac:

I trusted him. My father always walked with God.

But I started noticing — something was missing.

We had wood. We had fire. But no lamb.

Host:

You asked him?

Isaac:

I did. I said, *"My father... where is the lamb?"*

And he looked me in the eye and said,

"God will provide Himself a lamb."

That was all I needed to hear.

That was covenant faith talking.

Host:

Then came the altar.

Isaac:

Yes. He tied me. Laid me down. Raised the knife.

But listen — I didn't fight. I didn't run.

I believed what he said: *God will provide.*

And just before the blade came down, we heard a voice.

Host:

God spoke.

Isaac:

He said, *"Lay not thine hand upon the lad."*

Then we looked up — and there was a ram caught in the thicket.

214

God didn't just speak; He supplied.

Host:
You were part of something that revealed the heart of God.

Isaac:
Yes. I was the shadow of what was to come.
Years later, another Son would carry wood up a hill.
But there wouldn't be a ram that time.
Jesus became the Lamb — for all of us.

The Big Truth

1. God Doesn't Just Test the Parent — He Tests the Promise
Genesis 22:2 — "Take now thy son... and offer him."
Isaac wasn't just Abraham's son; he was the future.
God tested the very thing He promised.

2. Obedience Without Understanding Is Still Worship
Isaac didn't get the full picture, but he laid down anyway.
That's trust at its highest level.

3. Provision Is Already in Place Before the Knife Ever Falls
Genesis 22:13 — "Behold, behind him a ram caught in a thicket."
The sacrifice was already there — they just had to keep walking.

4. Your Sacrifice May Be a Symbol of Something Bigger
Isaac foreshadowed Jesus — both carried wood, walked up the hill,
and trusted the Father.

215

The difference? Jesus became the final offering.
John 1:29 — "Behold the Lamb of God..."

Closing Prayer

Father,
Sometimes I don't understand the test.
But help me to trust You anyway.

If You call me to lay down what I love,
let me do it with faith, not fear.
Let me believe, like Isaac, that You will provide.

I may not always see the ram in the thicket,
but I will walk, I will climb, and I will worship.

You are **Jehovah-Jireh**, the God who provides.
In Jesus' name, Amen.

End of Episode 33

The knife never fell, but faith never wavered.
On that mountain, obedience met mercy, and a ram was
waiting in the thicket.
Abraham didn't just pass the test — he discovered a Name.

Next Time on Late Night with the Word

He wasn't just a moment of provision;
He was a revelation of God's character.

In Episode 34, we sit down with **Jehovah-Jireh — The
God Who Provides.**

When you trust Him completely,
He reveals Himself faithfully.

Episode 34 | Jehovah Jireh — The God Who Provides

Theme: *He doesn't just make a way — He is the way.*

Scripture: *Genesis 22 : 14 (KJV)*

"And Abraham called the name of that place Jehovah-jireh: as it is said to this day, In the mount of the Lord it shall be seen."

Opening Monologue

There are names we give out of habit,
and then there are names we discover through experience.

Jehovah Jireh wasn't a title Abraham read in a scroll.
It was a truth he *learned* when everything was on the line.

The mountain wasn't just a test — it was a stage.
And in front of no audience but Heaven,
God showed up — not late, not early, but right on time.

The ram wasn't random.
The name wasn't forced.
And the moment wasn't small.

Tonight, we're not just talking about what God *did*.
We're sitting with **who He is.**

Guest of the Night: Jehovah Jireh — The God Who Provides

He doesn't run out.
He doesn't forget.
And He never shows up empty-handed.

Please welcome — **Jehovah Jireh.**

219

Interview: Host & Jehovah Jireh

Host:
Jehovah Jireh, welcome.
For so many, provision means money or resources,
but for You, it's deeper.
What does Your name really mean?

Jehovah Jireh:
It means *I see.*
I see the need before it appears.
I see the heart behind the obedience.
I see the moment before it reaches the mountain.
Provision is not about catching up — it's about being ahead.

Host:
Abraham was prepared to give up his son.
Why wait until the very last moment?

Jehovah Jireh:
Because faith must be walked out fully.
Provision isn't meant to interrupt faith — it's the reward of
it.
I let him climb with the question,
so he could descend with the answer.

Host:
That ram caught in the thicket — was it always part of the
plan?

Jehovah Jireh:
It was waiting before Abraham arrived.

What I provide is never reaction — it's orchestration.
The ram wasn't a backup plan.
It was *the* plan.

Host:
Why reveal this name at that precise moment?

Jehovah Jireh:
Because Abraham needed to know
that I am more than a promise-giver — I'm the promise-keeper.
Provision is My *character,* not just My *action.*
When you know Me as Jireh,
you stop panicking over what you cannot see.

Host:
What would You say to someone who feels forgotten?

Jehovah Jireh:
I have never missed a moment.
My silence is not absence.
My timing is not delay.
I see what you cannot,
and I move when it matters most.
Trust Me. I am still Jireh.

The Big Truth

1. God Sees Before He Provides
The name *Jehovah Jireh* means *"The Lord will see to it."*
What you think He missed, He already made a way for.

2. Provision Is Not Just Material — It's Personal
God didn't send gold. He sent a ram — the exact answer for the exact moment.
That's not supply; that's love.

3. Faith Walks Up What Fear Wants to Run Down
Abraham climbed with uncertainty but trusted anyway.
Provision meets those who keep walking.

4. God's Nature Doesn't Change at the Top of the Mountain
He was the same at the altar as He was in the promise.
The test was hard — but the Provider was faithful.

5. When You Remember the Name, You'll Never Forget the Moment
Abraham didn't name the place *Pain* or *Sacrifice*.
He named it *The Lord Will Provide*.
That's not just memory — that's worship.

Closing Prayer

Father,
I declare that You are **Jehovah Jireh — my Provider.**
You see what I cannot,
and You make a way I could never imagine.

I will not fear the climb or the cost.
What You require, You also supply.
My trust isn't in the ram — it's in the One who sends it.

You are faithful.
You are enough.
You are Jireh.

In Jesus' name, Amen.

End of Episode 34

Abraham looked up and saw it — the answer waiting the whole time.
A ram caught in the thicket — not by accident, but by assignment.
The test revealed the Name,
but the thicket revealed the grace.

Next Time on *Late Night with the Word*

We speak with **the Ram in the Thicket** — positioned by God,
caught for a purpose, and sent as a substitute.

This is more than a story — it's a shadow of the Cross.

Bonus Episode: The Ram in the Thicket — Caught on Purpose

Theme: *Caught on purpose*
Genesis 22:13 (KJV) — *"And Abraham lifted up his eyes, and looked, and behold behind him a ram caught in a thicket by his horns."*

Opening Monologue

It wasn't just a ram.
It was redemption in waiting.

Abraham lifted his eyes, and there it was—an answer no one expected—caught by the head, held in place by divine intent.

This wasn't luck. It wasn't chance. It was **placement.**
Because when obedience climbs, grace meets it.

Tonight, we sit with the one who took Isaac's place—the one who stood still when it could have run—the **ram caught in the thicket, and caught for a reason.**

Guest of the Night: The Ram in the Thicket

He didn't run.
He didn't fight.
He stood in the gap.

Please welcome **The Ram in the Thicket.**

Host:
Ram, thank you for being here. You weren't just in the right place at the right time—you were *placed.* Do you remember
225

how you got there?

Ram:

I didn't wander up the mountain; I was led. There was something pulling me—a sense that I had an appointment. When I reached the top, my horns got caught. It looked like a trap, but it was purpose.

Host:

Did you know you were going to die?

Ram:

Yes—but not for nothing. I felt it in my bones: I wasn't dying in vain. I was dying so someone else wouldn't have to. That's not loss—that's honor.

Host:

There are people who feel like they're stuck right now—like they're caught in something they didn't choose. What would you say to them?

Ram:

Just because you're caught doesn't mean you're forgotten. Sometimes what looks like limitation is actually divine positioning. Stay still. God might be using your moment to save someone else.

Host:

Wow. So you were more than an animal—you were a symbol.

Ram:

Yes—a symbol of grace, a shadow of something greater. I took Isaac's place, but Someone greater would come to take the place of all.

The Big Truth

1. The ram wasn't late—it was prepared.
God didn't scramble to find a substitute. The ram was ready before Abraham arrived.

2. Substitution is a picture of salvation.
Just as the ram took Isaac's place, Jesus became the Lamb who takes away the sin of the world.

3. Obedience unlocks what is already provided.
Abraham didn't see the ram until he obeyed. Sometimes provision isn't revealed until the last step is taken.

4. eing caught can be divine.
What holds you might be what God uses. The thicket didn't trap the ram—it positioned him.

5. God provides not just to rescue but to reveal.
The mountain became a mirror of God's heart. Jehovah Jireh isn't just about giving—it's about showing us His love.

Closing Prayer

I declare that what looks like a trap may be divine positioning.
I trust Jehovah Jireh to provide—not just what I want, but what is needed.
Like the ram, I choose to stay available, even when I feel caught.
May I be part of someone else's redemption story.
And may I always remember that what God provides is never random—
it's always right on time.

227

In Jesus' name, Amen.

End of Bonus Episode.

Next Time on Late Night with the Word...

She waited for her husband's blessing but received it from God instead.
Rebekah is coming.
Let's talk courage, covering, and what it means to say yes to a destiny you didn't see coming.

Episode 35 | Rebekah — Chosen at the Well, Covered by the Word

Theme: *When you're in the right place, you don't have to fight for what's yours — God will send it to you.*

Scripture: *Genesis 24 : 15*

"And behold, Rebekah came out…"

Opening Monologue

Tonight's guest didn't audition to be chosen.
She wasn't campaigning to be someone's wife.
She was simply *serving* — watering, working, doing the ordinary —
when destiny walked up with **camels and confirmation**.

She offered a stranger water and walked away with *jewelry, prophecy,*
and a place in the **lineage of Christ**.

She didn't beg for the blessing — she was *prepared* for it.
Because when purpose is looking for you, service is how it finds you.

Let's talk timing, trust, and being ready when the call comes.
Please welcome to the stage — **Rebekah.**

Interview: Host & Rebekah

Host:
Rebekah! The woman who was literally at the right place at the right time.
Welcome to *Late Night with the Word.*

230

Rebekah:

Thank you! I wasn't looking to be chosen — I was just
going to get water.

Host:

Walk us through that day. You go to the well, and then what?

Rebekah:

I saw a man with camels. He asked me for a drink.
I gave him one, then offered to water all his camels too.
I didn't know who he was, or that I was answering a specific
prayer.
I was just doing what I do — serve.

Host:

And because of your generosity, you became the answer to
his prayer.

Rebekah:

Exactly. He had just prayed, *"Let the one who offers to
water the camels
be the one You've chosen for Isaac."*
I was moving in kindness, but God was moving in covenant.

Host:

Then he gives you bracelets, earrings, and reveals who he is.

Rebekah:

My life changed in moments.
He said I was chosen to marry Isaac — Abraham's son.
It was a lot to take in, but my spirit knew: *this was divine.*

Host:
And when your family asked if you'd go, you didn't hesitate.

Rebekah:
I said, *"I will go."*
Sometimes, when God sends the opportunity, you don't need more details —
you just need *faith.*

Host:
And then you met Isaac, walking in the field.

Rebekah:
Yes. I covered myself with a veil.
I didn't need to be *seen* first — I needed to be *spiritually aligned.*
And Isaac welcomed me, loved me, and brought me into covenant.

The Big Truth

Rebekah wasn't in the palace — she was at the well.
She didn't push her way into purpose — she *flowed* into it.

1. God Uses Service to Open Supernatural Doors
Genesis 24 : 19 — "I will draw water for thy camels also."
She didn't know she was answering a prayer — she just served.
God watches how you move when nobody's watching.

232

2. The Right Heart Will Always Attract the Right Favor

She was chosen because of her *posture,* not her position.
Humility and kindness are the magnet of divine connection.

3. Obedience Without Full Understanding Leads to Blessing

Genesis 24 : 58 — "Wilt thou go with this man? And she said, I will go."
She didn't demand proof; she discerned her moment.
Faith doesn't wait for the full picture — it moves when God calls.

4. God Doesn't Forget the Faithfully Hidden

Rebekah wasn't performing for attention — she was *drawing water.*
When the time came, God revealed her to the right one.
The hidden faithful are the first found by heaven.

Prayer

Father,
Thank You for reminding me that I don't have to force favor.
When I'm in position, You'll send what's meant for me.

Teach me to serve faithfully, love humbly, and listen when You say, *Go.*
Let my obedience open doors that striving never could.
Keep me content in the well-season, and confident in Your timing.

I don't need to be everywhere — just where You've assigned

233

me.
And when destiny calls, give me the courage to say, *I will go.*

In Jesus' name,
Amen.

End of Episode 35

She came to the well with a pitcher,
and left carrying a promise.
No striving. No scheming. Just readiness.

When service met destiny, the covenant began to flow.

Next Time on *Late Night with the Word*

He fought for his brother's blessing,
but found his *own* along the way.

Jacob is coming.
Let's talk *wrestling, identity,*
and what happens when **grace grabs the heel.**

Episode 36 | Jacob — The Wrestler and the Name Change

Theme: *You might have come into the world fighting, but God still has a new name for you.*

Scripture: *Genesis 32 : 28 —*

"Thy name shall be called no more Jacob, but Israel."

Opening Monologue

Tonight's guest was **born reaching**.
He came out *grabbing his brother's heel* and spent years trying to catch up.

He lied. He ran. He tricked — and got tricked.
He worked for love, lived in his brother's shadow, and crossed more than one line.

But then came **the moment** — alone on a riverbank.
One long night. One divine fight. One name change.

This is the story of struggle turned into strength — of a man who wrestled and walked away with a limp *and a blessing.*

Give it up for the man formerly known as Jacob — **Israel** is in the studio.

Interview | Host & Jacob

Host:
Jacob — heel-grabber, wrestler, survivor — welcome to *Late Night with the Word.*

Jacob:

236

Glad to be here. Took me a while — had to limp in.

Host:
(Laughs) Let's start there. You've had quite the journey.
What was it like being born behind Esau?

Jacob:
I felt like second place from the start.
I came out grabbing, and honestly — I never stopped.
I wanted the birthright, the blessing, the validation.

Host:
So you tricked your father and stole the blessing.

Jacob:
I did. I lied, pretended to be Esau. It worked — but it broke everything.
I had to run. That moment haunted me.

Host:
Then you ended up working for Laban.

Jacob:
For years. Got tricked myself — married Leah when I wanted Rachel.
It felt like I was reaping what I'd sown.
But even there, God didn't leave me.

Host:
Then came the wrestling match — one night, alone. What happened?

Jacob:
I was afraid. I was going back to face Esau.
I sent everything ahead — family, flocks — and I was alone.
Then suddenly I was fighting. I didn't know who it was at

first,
but I realized — this was Heaven.
I held on and said, *"I will not let You go unless You bless me."*

Host:
And He asked your name.

Jacob:
Yes. That question broke me.
He didn't ask because He didn't know — He asked so I would admit it.
I said, *"Jacob."* Deceiver. Manipulator. Hustler.
And He said, *"Not anymore. Your name is Israel, for you have wrestled with God and with man, and have prevailed."*

Host:
So the limp was a mark?

Jacob:
Absolutely. I walked away wounded but different — changed, marked.
I've been limping with purpose ever since.

The Big Truth

Jacob's story proves that **God doesn't bless the perfect — He blesses the persistent.**

1. What You Grab Early Can't Compare to What God Gives Later
Jacob grabbed his brother's heel, but later wrestled Heaven itself and received a better blessing.

238

You don't have to steal what God has already promised.

2. Your Struggle Isn't Your End — It's Your Identity Shift
Genesis 32 : 28 — "Your name shall be Israel."
Jacob didn't just get a blessing — he got a new name.
New names come from **encounters**, not effort.

3. God Will Wrestle You Into Surrender
That night wasn't about defeating Jacob; it was about *breaking him into purpose.*
Sometimes the limp becomes your loudest testimony.

4. Even When You've Messed Up, God Still Has a Nation in You
He started as a deceiver, but Israel became the father of tribes.
That's what grace does — it turns a mess into a movement.

Prayer

Father,
I've wrestled. I've run. I've tried to do it my way.
But I don't want to live under the wrong name anymore.

Call me by who I really am.
Break what needs to be broken.
Bless what You've placed inside me.

And when I walk away, let me be changed forever.

239

I may limp — but I'll never be the same.

In Jesus' name,
Amen.

End of Episode 36

He wrestled with God and walked away different.
His limp was proof of his encounter,
and his new name was proof of his destiny.

Next Time on *Late Night with the Word*

He was the firstborn — the hunter, the strong one.
He lost the birthright, missed the blessing, and cried out in anguish.
But when the moment came to face the brother who deceived him,
he chose **forgiveness over fury.**

Esau steps onto the stage.
Let's talk *loss, legacy,* and how healing can happen — even when the blessing didn't.

Episode 37 | Esau — The Blessing I Lost and the Forgiveness I Found

Theme: *Just because you were wounded doesn't mean you have to stay bitter.*

Scripture: *Genesis 33 : 4 —*

"And Esau ran to meet him, and embraced him, and fell on his neck, and kissed him; and they wept."

Opening Monologue

Tonight's guest came out first — strong, red, hairy, and ready to lead.
He was the **original heir**, the **firstborn**, the one meant to carry the blessing.

But it all shifted — over a bowl of stew, a disguised brother, and a moment that changed everything.
He cried out for the blessing with everything he had — and still didn't get it.

Yet instead of letting bitterness define him, he let **forgiveness** free him.

Let's talk pain, pressure, and what it looks like to move forward when what's yours gets handed to someone else.
Esau is in the building.

Interview | Host & Esau

Host:
Esau — firstborn, the one who lost it all and somehow still walked in peace — welcome.

242

Esau:

Thank you. It took a long time to heal enough to talk about it.

Host:

Let's start with that moment. Your father's dying, you go to make his favorite meal, and when you come back — Jacob's already taken the blessing. What did that do to you?

Esau:

I broke. I cried out, *"Bless me too, Father!"* But it was too late.

He'd already given the covenant away. It felt like everything I was born for got stolen in a single moment.

Host:

And it wasn't just the birthright — it was identity, inheritance, legacy.

Esau:

Exactly. And it wasn't just one thing — it was a pattern. Jacob took the birthright when I was hungry, then the blessing when I wasn't looking.

I wanted revenge.

Host:

You even said, *"As soon as our father dies, I'll kill him."* But years passed, and something changed.

Esau:

Time changed me. God changed me.

I built my own. I had a family, a future.

And when I saw Jacob again after all those years — I didn't run to fight.

I ran to forgive.

243

Host:
That moment in *Genesis 33* — you wept on his neck. That wasn't weakness; that was healing.

Esau:
Exactly. I realized: the blessing may have skipped me, but **bitterness wouldn't own me**.
I let it go — and I let God write my next chapter.

The Big Truth

Esau didn't get the blessing from Isaac,
but he still received abundance from God.

1. You Can Be Done Wrong and Still Walk in Peace
Genesis 27 : 38 — "Hast thou but one blessing, my father?"
He begged for it. But what Isaac couldn't give, God still worked out.

2. Bitterness Will Chain You to a Past That Forgiveness Can Set You Free From
Esau could've lived angry forever,
but he chose to break the cycle.
Ephesians 4 : 31 — "Let all bitterness be put away from you."

3. Even Without the Birthright, Esau Was Still Blessed
Genesis 36 : 7 — "Esau was rich; the land could not contain them both."
Sometimes the blessing isn't in what you get — it's in who

244

you become after the loss.

4. Forgiveness Doesn't Mean You Weren't Hurt — It Means You Won't Stay Bound

Esau wept, but he didn't swing.
He hugged what hurt him — and walked away whole.

Prayer

Father,
I've been wronged. I've lost things I thought belonged to me.
But today — I give You the pain.

I won't live bitter.
I won't chase revenge.
I won't carry hate when You've called me to peace.

Let me be like Esau.
Let me cry if I have to — but let me forgive and walk free.

In Jesus' name,
Amen.

End of Episode 37

Esau didn't just eat; he exchanged **destiny for a dish.**

Bonus Episode | Lentil Soup — The Price of a Birthright

Theme: *When appetite outruns purpose*

Scripture: *Genesis 25 : 34 (KJV)* —

"Then Jacob gave Esau bread and pottage of lentils; and he did eat and drink, and rose up, and went his way: thus Esau despised his birthright."

Opening Monologue

Not every loss is loud.
Some happen quietly — at the dinner table.

Esau didn't storm out of the promise.
He *sat down* and gave it away.

It wasn't murder or betrayal — it was **hunger**.
And in a single moment, a bowl of lentils became more important than a future of favor.

Tonight, we talk to what was in that bowl.
Because this isn't just about food — it's about what people give up when their stomach speaks louder than their spirit.

Please welcome **the Lentil Soup**.

Interview | Host & Lentil Soup

Host:
Soup, thanks for joining us. People have eaten stew for centuries, but your moment with Esau was different. What happened that day?

Lentil Soup:

I didn't ask to be part of it. I was just simmering, doing what I was made to do.

But when Esau came in from the field — tired and impulsive — he didn't care what I cost.

He just wanted what was easy.

Host:

So you weren't the problem — the hunger was.

Lentil Soup:

Exactly. Hunger isn't wrong, but when it speaks louder than wisdom, it becomes dangerous.

Esau could've waited. He could've cooked.

But he chose me over what was already his — a birthright.

Host:

Some might say it wasn't a big deal — just a meal. How would you respond?

Lentil Soup:

It's never *just* a meal when destiny is on the table.

Esau thought he was making a small choice, but small choices become heavy when they touch purpose.

He walked away full — but empty.

Host:

What do you represent to people today?

Lentil Soup:

I represent every impulsive decision that feels good now but costs you later — the relationship you knew wasn't right, the opportunity you took without praying.

I'm the shortcut, the substitute, the soft voice that says, *"Take it now,"* while God whispers, *"Wait, I have more."*

248

The Big Truth

Convenience Can Be Costly
Esau chose what was quick over what was eternal.
The flesh loves shortcuts, but the spirit grows in surrender.

Not Every Appetite Is Worth Feeding
Hunger is natural, but what you reach for in those moments reveals who you trust.

Desire Without Discipline Leads to Regret
Esau didn't just lose his birthright — he despised it.
When you stop valuing what God gave, you risk trading it for what passes quickly.

Satisfaction Is Temporary; Consequences Are Not
Esau ate, drank, got up, and moved on — but the weight of that moment followed him for life.

There's Always Something Cooking — Make Sure It's Worth It
Not everything in the pot is from God.
Smell it. Test it. Ask the Spirit before you taste.

Closing Prayer

I declare that I will not trade my calling for comfort.
I will not exchange what is sacred for what is quick.

God, give me discernment when I'm hungry.
Teach me to wait when my flesh screams for more.

I will not despise the birthright You've placed on my life.
I will treasure it, protect it, and walk in it.

Let wisdom rise above impulse.
Let purpose rule over appetite.

In Jesus' name,
Amen.

End of Bonus Episode

She was promised to one man, married to another, and loved by neither — yet chosen by God.

Next time on **Late Night with the Word**:
Leah takes the mic.
Let's talk rejection, worth, and what it means to be *seen* even when you're *unloved.*

251

Episode 38 | Leah — Unloved But Chosen

Theme: *When man doesn't choose you—but God does.*

Scripture: *Genesis 29 : 31 —*

"And when the Lord saw that Leah was hated, He opened her womb."

Opening Monologue

Tonight's guest was given to a man who didn't want her. Married by deception. Loved in degrees. Left competing with the one who had his heart.

But while she fought for attention, **God gave her legacy.**

She may not have been Jacob's favorite—
but she was God's choice to birth praise, priesthood, and a King named Jesus.

This is for the overlooked. The one they walked past.
The one they used—but didn't love.
Because when God sees what they don't, **everything shifts.**

Please welcome **Leah.**

Interview | Host & Leah

Host:
Leah, welcome to the show. I want to start by saying this: *I see you. And so does God.*

Leah:
Thank you. That means more than you know.

Host:

Let's go back. Your father Laban switched you in on your sister Rachel's wedding night. What was that moment like?

Leah:

I wanted love—not trickery. I didn't ask to be part of a scheme, but I obeyed my father.
I went in covered, silent… and I woke up married to a man who didn't want me.

Host:

You were his wife—but not his choice.

Leah:

Yes. I watched him love Rachel openly.
And I tried to win him—with children.
One son after the next. Each name was a cry:
Maybe now he'll love me… maybe now he'll stay… maybe now he'll see me.

Host:

But something changed with your fourth son.

Leah:

It did. After Reuben, Simeon, and Levi, I said, *"This time, I will praise the Lord."*
And I named him **Judah.** That was my turning point.
I stopped birthing for a man and started birthing for my God.

Host:

Judah would become the line Jesus came from.

Leah:

Exactly. I wasn't the loved wife—but I was the chosen mother.
God saw my pain and turned it into a promise.

253

Host:

What would you say to women still trying to be picked?

Leah:

Stop trying to be seen by people who are blind to your value.
God sees. God hears. And God knows how to build
something royal out of rejection.

The Big Truth

Leah's story proves that being unwanted by man doesn't
cancel your assignment from God.

**1. You May Not Be Their First Choice—but You're Still
in God's Plan**
Genesis 29 : 31 — "When the Lord saw that Leah was
hated, He opened her womb."
Rejection made room for revelation.
God gave her fruitfulness in the face of favoritism.

2. What You Birth in Pain Can Still Carry Purpose
Each child was a season, a cry, a statement.
But when she birthed **Judah**, she birthed **praise**—and the
King of kings' bloodline.

3. God Doesn't Need You to Be Celebrated to Be Called
Leah wasn't celebrated, but she was consecrated.
God used her womb to usher in worship, leadership, and
redemption.

4. You Don't Need Their Validation When You're Walking in Vocation
The very thing people overlooked became the oil God used.

Prayer

Father,
Thank You for seeing what others miss.
Thank You for loving what others label.

I may not be everyone's first choice,
but I am **Yours.**

Help me release the need for validation.
Help me stop birthing for attention and start birthing for
Your glory.

Let praise rise from my pain.
Let purpose rise from rejection.
And let me remember, like Leah—
You still choose the ones nobody claps for.

In Jesus' name,
Amen.

End of Episode 38

She was beautiful, adored, and chosen—
but left empty, month after month, prayer after prayer.
While her sister birthed nations, she battled with
barrenness—until God remembered her.

Next time on Late Night with the Word:

Rachel is coming to the couch.
Let's talk longing, jealousy, and what happens when the
womb finally opens—but the wait has already changed you.

257

Episode 39 | Rachel — Loved, Waiting, and Remembered

Theme: *Even when it feels like you're last in line, God still remembers you.*

Scripture: *Genesis 30 : 22 —*

"And God remembered Rachel, and God hearkened to her, and opened her womb."

Opening Monologue

Tonight's guest had the heart of the man.
She was the one he worked fourteen years for—
the one who made his eyes light up, yet whose womb remained closed.

While her sister gave birth again and again, she was left to smile on the outside and suffer in silence.
But then came the shift—because God doesn't just open wombs;
He remembers cries, even the ones whispered through tears.

Please welcome the woman who waited in love but still had to be remembered.
Rachel is here.

Interview | Host & Rachel

Host:
Rachel, you were loved deeply but also hurt quietly. Thank you for being here.

Rachel:
Thank you. This story is still tender—but it's also testimony.

258

Host:
You were Jacob's choice. But while Leah birthed tribe after tribe, you were still waiting. How did that feel?

Rachel:
It felt like I was standing still while everyone else was moving.
I was loved, but I felt less than.
I smiled through ceremonies, but cried behind tents.
I watched child after child be born while I held empty arms.

Host:
You even told Jacob, "Give me children, or I die." That's heavy.

Rachel:
It was desperation. It wasn't just about babies—it was about worth.
In our culture, barrenness was shameful.
It felt like I had favor with man, but nothing from God.

Host:
Then came the moment—*God remembered you.*

Rachel:
Yes. It didn't come fast.
It came after jealousy, after frustration, even after trying to give Jacob my maidservant.
But eventually, **God remembered me.**
And I birthed **Joseph.** His name means *"The Lord shall add."*
Because I knew—He wasn't done yet.

The Big Truth

259

Rachel teaches us that delay is not divine dismissal.
God can love you deeply and still take His time.

1. You Can Be Loved and Still Longing
Rachel had Jacob's heart, but still carried empty arms.
It's okay to be grateful for what you have and still cry out
for what you're waiting on.

2. God Doesn't Just Hear—He Remembers
Genesis 30 : 22 — "And God remembered Rachel."
God didn't forget her—He waited for the perfect time.
And when He moved, He opened what no one else could.

3. You Don't Have to Compete to Be Seen
Rachel competed with Leah, but God wasn't grading her
against her sister.
He had her on her own divine timeline.
Comparison breeds confusion; trust brings peace and
promise.

4. Your First Blessing Is Just the Beginning
She birthed Joseph, but God had Benjamin in mind too.
When God starts a thing, He finishes it in fullness.

Prayer

Father,
I know what it feels like to be loved and still waiting—

to celebrate others while wondering, *When is it my turn?*

But today I hold on to Rachel's story.
You remembered her, and You'll remember me.
You haven't forgotten my tears.
You haven't missed my prayers.

And when You move, it will be perfect.
Open what only You can open.
And let my testimony sound like Joseph:
"The Lord shall add."

In Jesus' name,
Amen.

End of Episode 39

She was the bride he worked fourteen years to win—
but no scheme or struggle could outmaneuver God's timing.

Bonus Episode Next on Late Night with the Word:
We pull back the curtain on the man who rewrote the
wedding and renegotiated the blessing.
He was the uncle, the boss, the schemer—
but even his manipulation couldn't stop the movement of
God.

Laban is in the building.
Let's talk control, covenant, and what happens when a
master planner meets **the Master's plan.**

Bonus Episode: Host & Laban

Theme: *You can try to control the outcome, but you can't outwit the will of God.*
Genesis 31:29 (KJV) — *"It is in the power of my hand to do you hurt: but the God of your father spake unto me yesternight."*

Opening Monologue

Tonight's guest is a character.
He's the uncle, the employer, the wedding planner, and the negotiator.
He'll give you a deal—then switch it while you're sleeping.
He'll bless your business—then try to own your fruit.

But even the best manipulator can't outmaneuver the Master's plan.

He chased Jacob down with words, but was stopped by God's voice.
Please welcome to the studio the man who learned that schemes can't stop sovereignty—**Laban** is here.

Interview: Host × Laban

Host:
Laban, welcome. We've been waiting on you—though I'm guessing you'd say we agreed on someone else showing up.

Laban:
(Chuckles) Listen, I didn't lie—I just reordered a few things. Custom arrangements.

263

Host:

You gave Jacob Leah when he worked seven years for Rachel. Why?

Laban:

Because culture said the firstborn had to marry first. I was thinking legacy, order—and maybe a little leverage.

Host:

But you didn't tell him beforehand.

Laban:

Details! He still got Rachel—with a little extra work. Let's not forget, I made him wealthy too.

Host:

You also changed his wages ten times.

Laban:

He kept prospering! I figured if I could control the outcome, I could benefit from the blessing without giving up the source.

Host:

But God stepped in.

Laban:

He sure did. Spoke to me in a dream: *"Don't say anything good or bad to Jacob."*
That was my checkmate moment. I realized I might've been trying to manage God's man, but God had already managed the outcome.

The Big Truth

Laban shows us that **human control has limits, but God's**

covenant does not.

1. Manipulation Is Rooted in Fear of Losing Control
Laban didn't want to lose Jacob—or his blessings.
So he tried to control the situation through deceit.

Even When People Change the Terms, God Keeps the Covenant

Genesis 31:7 — "Your father hath deceived me, and changed my wages ten times; but God suffered him not to hurt me."
God will preserve what He promised, no matter who tries to block it.

2. You Can't Profit Off Someone Else's Promise Without Paying a Price
Laban benefited from Jacob's favor but didn't honor it.
Eventually, Jacob walked away with double.

3. God Will Speak to Your Enemies Before They Can Harm You

Genesis 31:24 — "And God came to Laban… saying, Take heed that thou speak not to Jacob either good or bad."
God's protection doesn't just surround you—it precedes you.

Closing Prayer
Father,
Thank You for showing me that I don't have to fear manipulative people.
You are my defender, my provider, and the One who keeps covenant.
Expose every scheme meant to delay my destiny.

265

Break every cycle of control—whether from others or in me.
And help me trust You more than I trust outcomes.
Let no Laban block what You've blessed.
In Jesus' name, Amen.

End of Bonus Episode.

Next Time on Late Night with the Word...

They didn't choose the spotlight.
They were handed to men, used to compete, asked to conceive.
But what they carried helped shape the twelve tribes of Israel.

Bilhah and Zilpah are stepping into the studio.
Let's talk silence, service, and what it means to be part of God's plan—even when history barely says your name.

Episode 40 | Host, Bilhah & Zilpah

Theme: *Even when history barely mentions your name, God still writes you into legacy.*

Scripture:

Genesis 30 : 3 — "And she shall bear upon my knees, that I may also have children by her."

Genesis 30 : 9 — "When Leah saw that she had left bearing, she took Zilpah her maid, and gave her Jacob to wife."

Opening Monologue

Tonight, we hand the mic to two women whose voices have been nearly lost in history.
They weren't chosen—they were *given.*
Not for love, but for legacy.

Used as surrogates in a battle between sisters,
but from their wombs came **Dan, Naphtali, Gad, and Asher**—
four tribes of a nation.

They labored without applause.
They birthed without titles.
But Heaven kept record.

Tonight, we honor the forgotten carriers of the promise.
Welcome to the show—**Bilhah and Zilpah.**

Interview | Host Bilhah Zilpah

Host:
Ladies, welcome. Your stories don't get much airtime, but your impact is undeniable.

Bilhah:
We weren't given a choice. We were handmaids—property. But even in that, *God saw us.*

Zilpah:
Our names may have been quiet, but our children carried purpose.
We weren't Rachel or Leah, but we were still part of the plan.

Host:
Let's talk about it. Bilhah—Rachel gave you to Jacob when she couldn't conceive. What was that moment like?

Bilhah:
It felt like my body was used, but my heart was ignored.
I carried a child—first Dan, then Naphtali—but it wasn't celebrated like a mother's joy.
It became part of a competition.

Host:
Zilpah, the same happened with you and Leah.

Zilpah:
Yes. Leah gave me to Jacob after she stopped bearing.
I gave birth to **Gad** and **Asher.**
And though I was behind the scenes, I knew what I carried mattered.

Host:

269

Looking back, what would you say to others who feel like they're just a means to someone else's win?

Bilhah:
You may be silent, but you're seen.
Even if man doesn't honor your role, God honors your sacrifice.

Zilpah:
Your purpose isn't always public.
But what you birth in silence, God multiplies in legacy.

The Big Truth

Bilhah and Zilpah teach us that you don't have to be in the spotlight to be in the story.

1. Even When You're Not the Headliner, You're Still in the Lineage
Genesis 35 : 22 – 26 lists all twelve tribes of Israel— including **Dan, Naphtali, Gad, and Asher.**
These women birthed nations quietly,
but their sons carried covenant weight.

2. Service Doesn't Cancel Significance
They were given, not chosen—
but God still counted what they carried.

3. You May Labor in Silence, But Heaven Keeps Record
Heaven remembers names the world skips.

There's a tribe in every hidden labor.

4. Purpose Isn't Always Loud — But It's Always Powerful
Some of the most meaningful impact comes from people no one applauds.
But God still builds legacy through their quiet *yes*.

Prayer

Father,
Thank You for **Bilhah** and **Zilpah**—
for reminding me that being unseen doesn't mean I'm unimportant.
Even when I'm behind the scenes, You still see what I carry.

Use my life to birth purpose, even if no one claps for it.
Let me labor with love, serve with strength, and trust You with the fruit.
Because You use handmaids to build nations—
and I say *yes,* even from the shadows.

In Jesus' name,
Amen.

End of Episode 40

They may not have been chosen for love,
but they were chosen for lineage.
Their quiet obedience became the roots of a nation.

Next on Late Night with the Word...

He was favored, gifted, and hated for what he carried.
They stripped his coat, threw him in a pit, and thought it was over—
but dreams don't die in dark places.

Joseph is stepping into the spotlight.
Let's talk betrayal, destiny, and what it means to be chosen for greatness,
even when it costs you everything.

273

Episode 41 | Host & Joseph

Theme: *When the dream looks dead, but destiny is still alive.*

Scripture: *Genesis 50 : 20 (KJV)* — "But as for you, ye thought evil against me; but God meant it unto good."

Opening Monologue

Tonight's guest wore favor like a coat—and it cost him everything.
He had a dream from God.
But instead of applause, he faced betrayal.
Instead of elevation, he found a pit.
Instead of justice, he was thrown into prison.

Yet what his enemies didn't know was this:
God never needed him in the crowd—He needed him in position.

Because favor doesn't skip pain;
it sustains you *through* it.

Please welcome the dreamer who went from betrayed to crowned—
Joseph is here.

Interview | Host Joseph

Host:
Joseph! You've got one of the most dramatic arcs in all of Scripture. Let's start with the dream.

274

Joseph:

I was young—seventeen. God showed me images: sheaves bowing, stars aligning.

I thought my family would celebrate.

Instead, they were offended.

Host:

Your brothers threw you into a pit.

Joseph:

Yes. They stripped me of my coat—the outward sign of favor.

But they couldn't strip the calling.

I went from a pit… to being sold… to serving in Potiphar's house.

Host:

And from there, accused and imprisoned.

Joseph:

For something I didn't do.

Even in prison, I helped others—interpreting dreams, encouraging faith.

But I was forgotten. Two full years passed before Pharaoh called my name.

Host:

But when the call finally came—

Joseph:

I was ready.

I went from prisoner to prime minister in one conversation.

God had been preparing me in the dark for what He was about to reveal in the light.

Host:

You met your brothers again years later. And instead of revenge—

Joseph:
I forgave them.
I told them, *"You meant it for evil, but God meant it for good."*
Every pain was positioning.
God didn't just save me—He used me to save many.

The Big Truth

Joseph's story reminds us that favor doesn't prevent pain—it *always* leads to purpose.

1. Just Because You're Favored Doesn't Mean You'll Be Understood
Genesis 37 : 8 — "Shalt thou indeed reign over us?"
Joseph didn't ask to be the favorite. He didn't ask to dream.
But favor often attracts resistance.

2. The Pit Is a Setup, Not a Sentence
The pit wasn't the end; it was a transition point.
Sometimes God allows you to be thrown down
so He can raise you up—*in His time.*

3. Delay Doesn't Mean Denial
Genesis 41 : 14 — "Then Pharaoh sent and called Joseph."
Joseph waited years, but when God said it was time,
the door swung wide open.

4. Your Pain Will Become Someone Else's Rescue
Genesis 50 : 20 — "God meant it for good, to save much people alive."
Joseph's story was never just about him.
Your survival isn't selfish—it's strategic.

Prayer

Father,
Thank You for Joseph's story—proof that the pit is not the end.
Thank You for showing me that what the enemy means for evil,
You can still use for good.

Help me trust You in the pit, serve You in the prison,
and represent You in the palace.
Remind me that the dream still lives—
and You will finish what You started.

In Jesus' name, **Amen.**

End of Episode 41

Before the pit and the pain, there was a gift—
a coat stitched in love, worn in favor,
and hated for what it represented.

Next time on Late Night with the Word...
We interview **the Coat of Many Colors.**
It didn't just cover Joseph—
it *revealed* him.

Episode 42 | The Coat of Many Colors — The Covering That Caused Conflict

Theme: *Favor can be seen before it is understood.*

Scripture: *Genesis 37 : 3 (KJV)* — "Now Israel loved Joseph more than all his children, because he was the son of his old age: and he made him a coat of many colours."

Opening Monologue

Not all battles start with betrayal—some start with favor.
Joseph didn't ask for the coat. He didn't choose it. It was **given**.
Stitched with intention, dyed with distinction, and placed on his shoulders by a father who saw something the others couldn't.

But the moment Joseph wore it, something shifted.
Brothers became bitter.
Eyes began to watch him differently.

What should have been a covering became a target.
Yet even when the coat was stripped from him, **the favor wasn't.**

Tonight, we interview the **Coat of Many Colors**—
the garment that represented love, destiny, and identity—
and the one that caught the attention of everyone around it.

Guest of the Night | The Coat of Many Colors — The Covering That Caused Conflict

Woven by a father's hands.

279

Misunderstood by jealous eyes.
Please welcome…the **Coat of Many Colors.**

Host:
Welcome, Coat. You've been called beautiful, dangerous, even divisive.
What was your purpose when Jacob made you?

Coat:
My purpose was love.
I wasn't created to provoke; I was created to cover.
Jacob didn't make me for conflict—he made me to represent favor.
I was his way of saying, *"This one carries something different."*

Host:
You've been blamed for what happened to Joseph. How do you respond?

Coat:
Favor is often misunderstood.
I didn't create the jealousy—I revealed it.
The brothers didn't hate me; they hated what I reminded them of.
Joseph wore me, but what they really saw was a future they couldn't understand.

Host:
When the brothers stripped you from Joseph and dipped you in blood, what did that moment feel like?

Coat:
Painful. Not for me, but for what I represented.

A lie was born that day.

A father's heart broke.

And a dreamer was buried—not by death, but by betrayal.

Yet even covered in blood, I still carried the memory of who he was.

Host:

You were never seen again in the story, but your impact remained.

What do you want people to understand about favor?

Coat:

Favor is not armor.

It won't stop the pit. It won't silence the jealousy.

But it *does* mark you.

You may be stripped, but you cannot be unchosen.

What God places on you may be removed from sight,

but it is never removed from your life.

The Big Truth

Favor is not earned—it is given.

Joseph didn't make the coat or request it; he simply received it.

The same is true for us. God's favor isn't a reward—it's a gift.

What you wear in the spirit may cause warfare.

The coat wasn't just physical—it was prophetic.

It represented destiny.

Sometimes the most visible signs of calling invite the greatest attacks.

Being stripped doesn't cancel what you carry.
Joseph lost the coat, but not the calling.
Even without the garment, the gift remained.
The pit couldn't take what God had placed within.

Envy sees favor as offense.
The brothers hated Joseph not for what he did, but for what he carried.
Some people are offended by what you didn't earn,
simply because they can't explain it.

The blood-stained coat wasn't the end of the story.
The coat was dipped in blood to signal death—
but Joseph was still alive.
That's the truth about God's chosen:
you can be written off, but still rise again.

Closing Prayer

I declare that what God has placed on me cannot be removed by people.
I will not fear favor.
I will wear what He gives me with humility and strength.
Even if I am misunderstood, I am not mistaken.
The same God who covered Joseph covers me.
And what He places on my life will reach the place He promised.

In Jesus' name, Amen.

End of Episode 42

The coat was stripped, but the calling remained.
Favor made him a target—and the next stop wasn't the palace; it was the **pit.**

Next time on *Late Night with the Word...*
We hear from **the Pit** that caught Joseph but couldn't keep him.
What does it mean when purpose falls before it rises?

Episode 43 | The Pit — The Place That Seemed Like the End

Theme: *The place where you were thrown can become the place where your purpose begins.*

Scripture: *Genesis 37 : 24 (KJV)* — "And they took him, and cast him into a pit: and the pit was empty, there was no water in it."

Opening Monologue

It's not the palace we remember first. It's the pit.
Before Joseph ever wore royal robes or stood in Pharaoh's court, he was thrown down into silence.

His brothers stripped him of the coat, plotted against him, tossed him aside, and walked away.
And all Joseph had left was a hole in the earth and a dream that felt buried.

But what if the pit was not punishment?
What if it was preparation?
What if the place you were left to die is the place where God begins to speak differently?

Tonight, we interview **the Pit** — the place of rejection, the start of Joseph's journey, and the silent witness to what men intended for evil but God would use for good.

Guest of the Night | The Pit — The Place That Seemed Like the End

It was deep, dry, and dark — but it was not forgotten.

Please welcome **The Pit.**

Host:

Pit, welcome. You're not usually seen as the hero of this story. How do you view your role?

Pit:

I was never meant to be a destination — I was a turning point.

Joseph didn't die in me; he discovered something in me.

He learned that being thrown away by man doesn't stop the plan of God.

Host:

Scripture says you were empty — no water. What does that say about what Joseph faced in that moment?

Pit:

He faced isolation. Silence. The absence of rescue.

But sometimes, it's in the dry places that dreams are refined.

I stripped him of everything but trust.

Host:

Were you the only pit in Scripture that carried that kind of weight?

Pit:

No. Many have passed through places like me.

Jeremiah was thrown into a dungeon.

David cried out from a horrible pit.

Jesus referenced Jonah in the belly of the fish — a pit of death.

But again and again, the pattern is the same: **God delivers.**

286

Host:
What would you say to someone who feels like they're in a pit season right now?

Pit:
Don't judge the story by this chapter.
I may feel final, but I am not the end.
Sometimes, God allows people to fall so they'll stop trusting the surface.
He's doing something deeper.
What begins in the pit may end in the palace.

Host:
And Joseph eventually rose from your depths into leadership.
What do you think when you look back on that?

Pit:
The pain made the purpose shine.
If Joseph hadn't come through me, he might not have had compassion for his brothers.
The pit helped form the man who would one day feed the same people who tried to kill him.

The Big Truth

The pit is not the promise — it's part of the process.
Joseph had a dream, but the pit felt like the opposite.
Still, God used it. Even your lowest moment can serve a higher purpose.

Emptiness does not mean absence.
The pit was empty of water, but not of destiny.
God still moves in dry places. His presence isn't measured

287

by what you see,
but by what He's doing behind the scenes.

You can be thrown down and still be chosen.
Joseph's brothers rejected him, but Heaven had already
selected him.
Man's rejection can't override God's election.

Many pass through the pit, but not all stay there.
The pit has held prophets, dreamers, and kings — but it
never kept them.
If God brought them out, He will do it for you.

Where man tried to bury, God began to build.
The pit was meant to silence Joseph's dream,
but instead it set the dream in motion.
What they thought was the end became the introduction
to the most powerful part of his journey.

Closing Prayer

I declare that the pit is not my grave — it is my preparation.
I will not let silence speak louder than the promises God
gave me.
I may be thrown down, but I am not cast away.
God sees me. God is with me.
And what begins in the pit will end in purpose.
I will rise.

End of Episode 43

The pit didn't end the story.
Hands reached in — but not to rescue, to sell.
What looked like betrayal was actually movement.

Next time on *Late Night with the Word* ...
We ride with the **Caravan** that carried Joseph to Egypt.
They thought they were delivering a slave,
but they were transporting a future ruler.

Episode 44 | The Caravan — The Carriers of Unexpected Destiny

Theme: *Just because someone sold you doesn't mean your value dropped.*

Scripture: *Genesis 37 : 28 (KJV)* — "Then there passed by Midianites merchantmen; and they drew and lifted up Joseph out of the pit, and sold Joseph to the Ishmeelites for twenty pieces of silver: and they brought Joseph into Egypt."

Opening Monologue

The pit was real.
The pain was deep.
But the story didn't stop there.

A group of merchants was on the road that day. Not prophets. Not priests. Just travelers—men with no clue they were helping fulfill prophecy. They pulled Joseph from the pit and placed him into a caravan headed for Egypt.

While the brothers thought they were getting rid of him, **God was positioning him.**

Because the ones who sold you do not control the outcome. They may have changed your location, but they did not cancel your assignment.

Tonight, we sit down with **the Caravan**—the unexpected transporters of purpose.

291

Guest of the Night | The Caravan — The Carriers of Unexpected Destiny

They didn't know who they were moving—but Heaven did. Please welcome, **The Caravan.**

Host:
Caravan, welcome. You were just passing by—or so it seemed. What really happened that day?

Caravan:
We were merchants—just on a route. But routes are never random when God is involved.
What looked like a sale was really a shift.
We didn't know the weight of who we carried, but Heaven did.

Host:
You moved Joseph from the pit to Egypt. Did you feel anything different?

Caravan:
We felt favor—not from man, but something we couldn't explain.
The boy we carried had purpose in his eyes, even in chains.
He didn't scream. He watched.
He was being moved—but not destroyed.

Host:
Many people see the sale of Joseph as betrayal. What do you represent in that moment?

Caravan:
We were proof that God can use even betrayal to fund the

journey.

Joseph wasn't sold to be forgotten—he was sent to be positioned.

God used ordinary movement to accomplish extraordinary prophecy.

Host:
You didn't just carry him—you delivered him.
What would you say to someone who feels like they're being taken somewhere they didn't ask to go?

Caravan:
If God allowed the movement, He's already prepared the arrival.
Egypt didn't see him coming—but Heaven did.
What feels forced may actually be divine transportation.

The Big Truth

You may be sold, but you are not worthless.
Joseph was traded for twenty pieces of silver, but that did not define his value.
What others give up on, God still uses.

Purpose does not die in transition.
The ride to Egypt wasn't the end of the dream—it was part of the journey.
Even when you're in motion, God is still in control.

God uses ordinary paths for extraordinary outcomes.
The merchants weren't prophets, but they were instruments.

God doesn't always move through the spectacular—sometimes He moves through the normal.

Your transportation may look like trouble, but it's really timing.
The caravan wasn't a prison—it was a path.
What looks like captivity may actually be protection for what's coming next.

God can use strangers to set you in position.
The brothers planned Joseph's removal, but the caravan carried him toward elevation.
Who touches you doesn't determine your future.
Who *sends* you does.

Closing Prayer

I declare that every move in my life is being used by God.
Even what felt like rejection will become redirection.
I am not lost—I am led.
The same God who carried Joseph from the pit to his purpose is guiding me.
And I will arrive exactly where He has planned for me to be.
Amen.

End of Episode 44

The pit didn't end the story—movement did.
What looked like betrayal became transportation.
What felt like loss became the road to leadership.

Next time on *Late Night with the Word* ...
His life saved a nation.
His bones carried a promise.
And he made them swear to carry him out, because Egypt wasn't the end.

Joseph returns one more time.
Let's talk legacy, death, and what it means to believe in promise *beyond your lifetime.*

Episode 45 | Host & Joseph (Legacy Edition)

Theme: *Legacy doesn't just leave instructions—it leaves faith behind.*

Scripture: *Genesis 50 : 25* — "... Ye shall carry up my bones from hence."

Opening Monologue

Tonight's guest has been here before.
He came with a coat. He came with a dream. He came with favor.

But now he's back—with a final request.
This time, he's not asking for a throne. He's not interpreting dreams.
He's asking for something deeper:
"When God moves you, take me with you."

Because legacy isn't about where you are—it's about where you know you're going.
He died in Egypt, but his faith lived all the way to Canaan.

Please welcome back the man who saw past his lifetime—
Joseph returns to the studio.

Interview | Host + Joseph (Legacy Edition)

Host:
Joseph, welcome back. The first time, you gave us dreams, survival, and strategy.
But this time—it's deeper.

297

Joseph:
Yes. Because after everything—rulership, reconciliation, restoration—
I still wasn't home.
Egypt sustained me, but it wasn't my final address.

Host:
You told your brothers, *"God will visit you, and when He does, take my bones with you."*
That's powerful.

Joseph:
It was a declaration of faith beyond breath.
I knew God wasn't done with us.
I didn't want to be buried in a place of survival;
I wanted to rest in the land of promise.

Host:
Legacy speaks—even in silence.

Joseph:
Yes. When they carried me out generations later, my bones preached.
They said: *He believed. He trusted. He waited.*
My final act was a faith move.

Host:
What would you tell people today who are trying to secure their future?

Joseph:
Don't just build for today—build for where God is taking your people.
Leave a trail of faith. Not just wealth. Not just memories.

298

But a spiritual path forward.

The Big Truth

Joseph didn't just live well—he died in expectation.
And that's what legacy really is: *prophetic faith with long-term vision.*

1. The Place That Sustains You May Not Be the Place That Fulfills You
Genesis 50 : 24 — "I die: and God will surely visit you."
Egypt was protection, but it wasn't promise.
Just because God places you somewhere doesn't mean it's permanent.

2. Legacy Means Making Room for a Future You May Never See
Joseph didn't witness the Exodus, but he spoke into it.
He gave the next generation a faith instruction.

3. Bones Don't Lie—They Testify
Exodus 13 : 19 — "Moses took the bones of Joseph with him."
Even Moses honored Joseph's faith.
Because real faith doesn't rot—it resonates.

4. You Don't Have to Be There to Lead Them Out
Joseph couldn't walk, but his bones moved.
Faith has a way of traveling long after you're gone.

Prayer

Father,
Teach me to live with vision bigger than my lifetime.
Let my choices echo in generations to come.
Let me leave more than words—let me leave faith.
Don't let me grow too comfortable in Egypt.
Even if You bless me there, remind me of the promise beyond.
And when my time comes,
let my life speak as loud in death as it did in life.
In Jesus' name, Amen.

End of Episode 45

Joseph's story doesn't end in Egypt—it ends in expectation.
His faith became a map, and his bones became a sermon.
Because legacy never stays buried; it always rises with the promise.

Next Time on *Late Night with the Word*

They were sons of Jacob—fierce, bold, and known for their wrath.
Their actions were impulsive, but not ignored.
One would be scattered.
The other would be transformed into a tribe of priests.

Levi and Simeon are stepping into the studio.
Let's talk anger, justice, and what happens when God rewrites your legacy.

Episode 46: Host, Levi & Simeon

Theme: Your past might scatter you, but God can still sanctify you.

Genesis 49:57 Simeon and Levi are brethren cursed be their anger, for it was fierce

Opening Monologue

Tonights guests were bold. Unapologetic. And deadly when they felt disrespected.

They didnt wait for permission,they acted.

When their sister was violated, they took vengeance into their own hands.

Their zeal led to slaughter. Their wrath led to consequences.

And their father Jacob never forgot what they did.

But thats not the end of the story.

Because one of these men went from a sword in his hand to a censer in the tabernacle.

Lets talk about passion, pain, and how God can take your rage and turn it into a calling.

Give it up for the sons of fire

Levi and Simeon are in the studio.

Interview: Host, Levi Simeon

Host:

Brothers,thank you both for coming. Your names? They carry heat.

Simeon:

Weve heard the stories. We lived them. Not all of them feel good.

Levi:

We acted out of rage. We didnt wait for Gods voice,we answered with swords.

Host:

This goes back to Dinah,your sister. She was violated, and you took matters into your own hands.

Simeon:

Shechem dishonored her. We werent thinking about mercy. We were thinking justice,our way.

Levi:

We made a plan. Said wed make peace if they were circumcised. But on the third day, we struck them down. Every man in that city. It was a bloodbath.

Host:

And your father, Jacob, said your anger was cursed

Simeon:

Yes. He said wed be divided and scattered. Our anger made us unstable.

Levi:

But God didnt leave it there. He couldve erased us,but He refined us. I was scattered,but I was also set apart. My tribe became the priests. The ones who carried the ark. Who stood between the people and the altar.

Host:

From violence to vessels.

Levi:

Yes. Because passion without direction is dangerous. But passion surrendered to God? Thats powerful.

The Big Truth

Levi and Simeon show us that God doesnt ignore your past,but He doesnt have to leave you there either.

1. Unhealed Passion Can Become Generational Pain

Genesis 49:7 Cursed be their anger I will divide them in Jacob, and scatter them in Israel.

Their decisions had consequences. They werent forgotten. But God still left space for redemption.

2. Zeal Without Gods Wisdom Is Destructive

They fought for justice,but not with righteousness.

304

Sometimes our motives are good,but our methods can wreck legacy.

3. God Can Scatter You and Still Set You Apart

Deuteronomy 10:8 At that time the Lord separated the tribe of Levi

Levi was scattered,but turned into the priesthood.

He didnt inherit land,he inherited presence.

4. Your Passion Isnt the Problem,Your Posture Is

God never took Levis fire,He just redirected it.

From a sword to a censer. From bloodshed to blessing.

Prayer

Father,

Thank You for showing me that even my mistakes have purpose.

Even my anger can be healed.

Even my fire can be holy.

Take every part of me,my emotions, my past, my pain,

and use it for Your glory.

I dont want to be driven by rage.

I want to be led by righteous fire.

Set me apart,just like You did with Levi.

And let my life go from reaction to reverence.

In Jesus name,

Amen.

End of Episode 46.

Next time on Late Night with the Word

He made mistakes. Big ones.

Sold his brother. Failed his family.

But somewhere in the middle of guilt and grief,God stirred up leadership.

He didnt start out strong, but he became the one to speak up, stand in the gap, and carry the promise.

Judah is stepping into the studio.

Lets talk failure, family, and what happens when praise rises from a broken place.

But thats not all...

Right after Judahs interview, were bringing in a Bonus Episode,

The woman who called him out and called him higher.

She was wronged, forgotten, and nearly burned for defending herself.

But her boldness preserved a bloodline, and her righteousness was recognized even by the man who betrayed

306

her.

Tamar is coming.

Lets talk survival, strategy, and what happens when God uses your pain to protect a promise.

Episode 47: Host & Judah

Theme: Your past may be messy,but God still calls you to lead.

Genesis 49:10 The sceptre shall not depart from Judah

Opening Monologue

Tonights guest doesnt have a squeakyclean record.

He made some choices that couldve canceled his name

But grace had other plans.

He sold his brother. Failed as a fatherinlaw. Fell into scandal.

And still? God stamped his name on the bloodline of Jesus.

This is the story of how praise can rise from regret and how leadership can grow in a heart that finally humbles itself.

Welcome to the stage the man whose mess didnt block the Messiah

Judah is in the building.

Interview: Host Judah

Host:

Judah. Theres so much to unpack with your story,thank you for coming.

Judah:

Thank you. It took me a while to realize Gods not afraid of my mess. He just needed my surrender.

Host:

Lets go back. You were the one who said, Lets not kill Joseph,lets sell him. What were you thinking?

Judah:

I wanted out of the guilt, but I didnt want blood on my hands. So I suggested we sell him. I thought I was doing better,but really, I was just covering cowardice.

Host:

And then came the Tamar situation

Judah:

That broke me. She called me out. Publicly. And I had to admit, She is more righteous than I am. That moment humbled me. It made me take a hard look at myself.

Host:

But then we see a shift years later, when Benjamins life is on the line, you speak up.

Judah:

I couldnt let another brother suffer. Not again. I told Joseph,before I even knew it was him,Take me instead. That was my redemption moment. That was my yes.

Host:

And then your father blesses you with the words The scepter shall not depart from Judah. From you came kings,and Christ.

Judah:

310

That blessing? It was bigger than me. God didnt choose me because I was perfect. He chose me because I was repentant. And He can always use a heart that turns back to Him.

The Big Truth

Judah proves that your past doesnt cancel your calling,in fact, it might prepare you for it.

1. Leadership Starts With Ownership

Genesis 38:26 She hath been more righteous than I

Judah didnt make excuses,he owned it.

Real leadership starts when you stop hiding and start healing.

2. God Can Turn a Schemer Into a Savior

Genesis 44:33 Now therefore let me abide instead of the lad

Judah stepped in and offered himself.

Thats transformation,from selfish to selfless.

3. Praise Doesnt Mean Perfection,It Means Presence

His name means praise. Not because he was always right,but because he always came back.

311

4. Messy Doesnt Mean Missed

Genesis 49:10 The sceptre shall not depart from Judah

God picked Judahs line for King David, and eventually Jesus.

If thats not redemption, I dont know what is.

Prayer

Father,

Thank You for Judahs story.

For showing me that You dont wait on perfection,you wait on repentance.

Use my voice. Use my leadership.

Use even my past,for Your glory.

Let praise rise from my pain.

Let legacy rise from my lowest point.

And let my yes be loud,even after my no messed up.

In Jesus name,

Amen.

Bonus Episode: Host & Tamar

Theme: When youve been wronged by the system but still chosen by God.

Genesis 38:26 She hath been more righteous than I

Opening Monologue

Tonights guest isnt your typical Bible heroine.

She didnt wait in the background.

She didnt keep quiet when injustice came knocking.

She risked shame, rejection, and even death all to protect a promise.

While the men around her broke their word, she kept the lineage alive.

She stood in the gap, not as a victim,but as a vessel of righteousness.

Please welcome to the show the woman who called out a patriarch and carried the line of the Messiah

Tamar is in the studio.

Interview: Host Tamar

Host:

Tamar. Your story,whew. Its layered. Thank you for being here.

Tamar:

314

Ive been misunderstood for centuries. But I didnt do what I did for attention,I did it for justice.

Host:

Lets go back. You were married to Judahs son, Er

Tamar:

Yes. He was wicked. The Lord took him. Then I was given to his brother Onan. But he refused to honor the law of levirate marriage. He used me, but didnt fulfill his duty.

Host:

And then Judah promised you his youngest son,Shelah,but never gave him to you?

Tamar:

Exactly. I waited faithfully. But I realized he never intended to keep his word. He was more concerned with reputation than righteousness.

Host:

So you took matters into your own hands

Tamar:

I covered my face. Sat by the roadside. And Judah,without knowing,came to me. I didnt do it to be scandalous. I did it to hold him accountable.

Host:

And when he found out?

Tamar:

He said, She hath been more righteous than I. That moment

315

flipped the script. I didnt just save my future,I preserved his lineage.

Host:

You had twins,Perez and Zerah. And Perez would become part of Jesus lineage.

Tamar:

From shame came salvation. You dont have to be perfect to be purposed.

The Big Truth

Tamar shows us that Gods plan wont be stopped by injustice, silence, or scandal,Hell use the brave to make history.

1. Dont Let Rejection Make You Forget the Promise

Tamar couldve given up after being passed over. Instead, she found a way to hold the system accountable.

2. Righteousness Isnt Always Neat

Genesis 38:26 She hath been more righteous than I

It wasnt a traditional path. But it exposed truth and preserved the line of Judah.

3. God Can Birth Legacy Out of Scandal

Matthew 1:3 And Judas begat Phares and Zara of Thamar

Shes one of only a few women listed in Jesus genealogy. Thats not accident,thats divine vindication.

4. When People Forget You, God Will Still Favor You

Tamar was cast aside,but God called her essential.

Prayer

Father,

Thank You for Tamar.

For reminding me that I dont have to be perfect to be used,just willing to stand in truth.

Give me courage when systems fail me.

Give me wisdom when people overlook me.

And let my boldness preserve what Youve promised.

When man forgets, let heaven remember.

In Jesus name,

Amen.

Bonus Episode

Next time on Late Night with the Word

One was the baby of the family,tender, protected, and deeply loved.

The other? A steady soul,silent, strong, and born to bear burdens.

Benjamin and Issachar are taking the stage.

Lets talk identity, inheritance, and what it means to walk in quiet strength and Godgiven

319

Episode 48: Host & Benjamin

Theme: You dont have to be loud to be powerful when youre led by love and walk in wisdom.

Genesis 49:1415 Issachar is a strong ass couching down between two burdens

1 Chronicles 12:32 And of the children of Issachar, which were men that had understanding of the times

Genesis 49:27 Benjamin shall ravin as a wolf

Opening Monologue

Tonights guests didnt need many words to carry weight.

One was the youngest son,born in sorrow, named in love, and favored in silence.

The other? A prophetic thinker. A quiet worker. A tribe known for knowing what time it was and what needed to be done.

They remind us that strength isnt always seen,and wisdom doesnt always shout.

Lets talk legacy, discernment, and the power of being in Gods timing even if the spotlight skips you.

Give it up for the quiet storm and the timing tribe

Benjamin and Issachar are here.

Interview: Host, Benjamin Issachar

Host:

Benjamin, Issachar,thank you both for being here. You two were quiet in Scripture,but deep in impact.

Benjamin:

Some of us carry favor in silence.

Issachar:

And some of us are assigned to watch and wait,until its the right time to move.

Host:

Benjamin, lets start with you. You were born to Rachel,her final act of love and pain. What does your name mean to you?

Benjamin:

She called me Benoni,son of my sorrow. But Jacob renamed me Benjamin,son of my right hand.

That shift reminds me that even if youre born in pain, you can still walk in power and position.

Host:

Genesis says youll ravin like a wolf. What does that mean to you?

Benjamin:

Theres a fight in me. I may have been the youngest,but I was never weak. I protect whats mine. I walk quietly,but if you threaten my tribe, I roar.

Host:

Now Issachar,your tribe became known for discerning the times. What did that look like?

Issachar:

We were observers. Learners. While others reacted, we reflected.

We didnt move off emotion,we waited for the divine window.

We understood seasons, timing, assignment.

Host:

And Scripture says you were like a donkey lying between burdens

Issachar:

People thought that meant low or passive. But really,it meant we carried weight with wisdom.

We knew when to speak and when to stay silent. We werent flashy,but we were foundational.

Host:

What would both of you say to people who feel hidden?

Issachar:

Being hidden doesnt mean youre not valuable. Sometimes God hides whats essential until the right moment.

Benjamin:

You dont have to be loud to be legendary. Just be faithful. God sees.

The Big Truth

Benjamin and Issachar teach us that discernment and loyalty can shake nations, even when theyre not the loudest in the room.

1. You Can Be Born in Sorrow and Still Walk in Strength

Genesis 35:18 She called his name Benoni but his father called him Benjamin.

God can rename what pain tried to define.

2. Understanding the Times is a Weapon of Warfare

1 Chronicles 12:32 The sons of Issachar understood the times and knew what Israel ought to do

We need discerners. People who dont just move,but move when God says move.

3. Being Quiet Doesnt Disqualify You from Destiny

Some of the strongest tribes were the ones you rarely heard from.

Because they werent loud,they were locked in.

4. God Will Give You a Seat at the Right Time

Issachars tribe advised kings. Benjamin produced warriors.

The hidden ones often carry the deepest weapons.

Prayer

Father,

Thank You for reminding me that I dont have to be loud to be heard by heaven.

Give me the wisdom of Issachar,to know the times.

Give me the strength of Benjamin,to move with purpose, not pressure.

Teach me to rest between burdens and rise when its time.

Let me not miss my moment. Let me not chase noise.

Let me be quiet, but effective.

In Jesus name,

Amen.

End of Episode 48.

Next time on Late Night with the Word

She didnt ask for what happened.

She was silenced, covered, and left out of the familys narrative.

But heaven still heard her cry.

Dinah is coming to the studio.

Lets talk identity, injustice, and what it means when your pain is written in the Word,even if your voice was never recorded.

325

Episode 49: Host & Dinah

Theme: Even when the world skips your voice, heaven still records your name.

Genesis 34:1 And Dinah went out to see the daughters of the land.

Opening Monologue

Tonights guest was never quoted in Scripture,but her pain was remembered.

She was a daughter in a house full of sons. A young woman who went to see the world

and was caught in a story of injustice, silence, and rage.

Her name is barely mentioned. Her words never recorded.

But her story still speaks to women everywhere whove been used, dishonored, and forgotten.

This is a safe space for the girl who was left out of the blessing

But not out of Gods memory.

Please welcome to the show Dinah.

Interview: Host Dinah

Host:

Dinah, thank you. Your story has been buried under

326

everyone elses pain,but tonight, we want to hear you.

Dinah:

Thank you. For years, Ive been the girl in the background of the scandal. But I wasnt just a daughter. I was a person.

Host:

You went out to see the daughters of the land and tragedy followed.

Dinah:

Yes. I went to observe, to learn, to see outside of my tent. But Shechem,the prince,took me. And the next thing I knew it was no longer a moment of curiosity. It became a moment of trauma.

Host:

And the aftermath?

Dinah:

I was brought home. But no one asked me what I felt. My brothers acted. My father stayed quiet. Decisions were made about me, but never with me.

Host:

Your brothers, Simeon and Levi, avenged you violently. Did that bring peace?

Dinah:

No. It brought blood. And silence. My pain was used to justify rage,but it didnt heal me.

And after that? I disappeared from the text. But I didnt

disappear from God.

Host:

What would you say to women today whove been violated and silenced?

Dinah:

You are not your trauma. You are not invisible. Even if people dont write your story,God still records every tear.

You are seen. You are valuable. And you will rise.

The Big Truth

Dinah reminds us that even in injustice, God sees. God remembers. And God heals.

1. Being Left Out Doesnt Mean Being Left Behind

Dinah wasnt named in the twelve tribes. But she was still Gods daughter.

Isaiah 61:3 ...to give unto them beauty for ashes.

2. What Happens to You Isnt Who You Are

Her identity was not her violation.

She was more than a moment,she was a whole soul with a future.

3. God Heals What Others Wont Touch

328

People may avoid your pain. They may walk around it or talk over it.

But God enters it,and restores from the inside out.

4. Your Story Matters, Even When Its Not Loud

Dinah didnt get chapters,but she got recognition.

And thats proof: God keeps record of every daughters pain and every daughters rise.

Prayer

Father,

Thank You for seeing me.

For hearing the cries I never said out loud.

For holding the pieces of my story that others ignored.

Heal me in the places where Ive been violated.

Speak to the wounds that no one wants to talk about.

And restore my voice,even if I whisper.

I am not forgotten. I am not shame.

I am Yours.

And You still write my story.

In Jesus name,

Amen.

End of Episode 49.

Next time on Late Night With the Word

He was forgotten, but still favored.

Locked up, but still carrying a gift.

In the dark corners of a prison, Joseph meets two men,one with a dream that leads to restoration, and one with a dream that leads to judgment.

The Cupbearer and the Baker are stepping into the studio.

Lets talk dreams, discernment, and what it means when God uses your gift even before your freedom comes.

Episode 50: The Cupbearer the Baker Dreams in the Dark

Theme: God still speaks in the prison, and your gift still works,even when youre waiting.

Genesis 40:8 Do not interpretations belong to God? Tell me them, I pray you.

Opening Monologue

Tonights guests werent kings or patriarchs.

They didnt lead armies, build altars, or receive covenant promises.

But their dreams,shared in a dark prison cell,became the very key that unlocked the palace door for one of the Bibles greatest deliverers.

They remind us that no moment is wasted, and that God is working behind the scenes,even in places that feel like punishment.

Please welcome to the studio, the men who dreamed their way into biblical history

The Cupbearer and the Baker.

Interview: Host, Cupbearer, and Baker

Host:

Gentlemen, thank you for joining us. You both held positions in Pharaohs court, and suddenly, you found yourselves in prison. What happened?

Cupbearer:

There was tension in the palace,something went wrong, and both of us were removed. No warning. One day were trusted servants, the next,were in chains.

Baker:

Everything we had was stripped. Reputation. Freedom. Hope. We didnt know what tomorrow looked like.

Host:

And then you both had dreams. Same night. What were those dreams like?

Cupbearer:

Mine was a vine with three branches. It budded, blossomed, and brought forth grapes. I took the grapes and placed them in Pharaohs cup.

Baker:

I dreamed of three baskets of bread on my head, but birds came and ate from the top basket. I woke up uneasy.

Host:

Joseph saw your faces and asked why you were sad,and then offered to interpret your dreams. What was that like?

Cupbearer:

It was strange. He was a prisoner like us, but he carried peace. He listened carefully. Then said, In three days youll be restored to Pharaohs court. And he was right.

Baker:

My interpretation was harder to hear. He said Id be executed in three days. I didnt want to believe it,but it came to pass.

Host:

Joseph asked you to remember him, Cupbearer, when you were restored. Did you?

Cupbearer (sighs):

Not at first. I was caught up in the return. I forgot until Pharaoh had a dream. Thats when it hit me,Theres a man in the prison who knows how to interpret dreams. That moment changed everything.

The Big Truth

Josephs time with the Cupbearer and Baker proves that God places purpose in every environment,even the prison.

1. God Will Give You a Gift That Works in Every Season

Josephs gift didnt just operate in the palace,it worked in the prison too.

Genesis 40:8 Do not interpretations belong to God?

2. Not Every Door Opens Immediately,But Every Seed Planted Will Be Remembered

Joseph interpreted and asked to be remembered. The Cupbearer forgot for a time.

But Gods timing was still perfect.

Genesis 41:9 Then spake the chief butler unto Pharaoh, saying, I do remember my faults this day

3. Even in Dark Seasons, You Can Be a Light

Joseph served others while he was still waiting on his own release.

He didnt let bitterness block his obedience.

4. One Divine Appointment Can Shift Your Entire Life

That one moment led to Joseph standing before Pharaoh,and ultimately, saving a nation.

Prayer

Father,

Thank You for reminding me that my gift still has value, even in places that feel hidden or forgotten.

Help me serve others while I wait.

Help me trust You when Im overlooked.

And help me stay faithful until You say, Now its time.

Let my obedience in the dark prepare me for the light.

In Jesus name,

Amen.

End of Episode 50.

Next time on Late Night with the Word

Before the prison before the dreams

There was a house. A promotion. A test.

He had favor with Potiphar, power over the house,

But one womans lie cost him his robe and his reputation.

Potiphar and his wife are entering the studio.

Lets talk temptation, false accusation, and what happens when integrity puts you in chains,but keeps you in purpose.

337

Episode 51: Host & Potiphar

Theme: You can lose your position and still keep your purpose when your integrity stays intact.

Genesis 39:12 And she caught him by his garment, saying, Lie with me: and he left his garment in her hand, and fled

Opening Monologue

Tonights guests were part of one of the most intense chapters in Josephs story.

He had finally risen from slave to manager.

He ran the entire estate. He was trusted. Successful. Covered in favor.

But favor attracted attention,and not all of it holy.

One woman, one lie, one stolen robe,and he was in chains again.

This is the story of how a false accusation set the stage for a divine appointment.

Give it up for the head of Pharaohs guard,and the wife who couldn't keep her hands to herself

Potiphar and his wife are here.

Interview: Host, Potiphar His Wife

Host (to Potiphar):

Potiphar, you trusted Joseph with everything. What made him stand out?

Potiphar:

He carried excellence. He was young, but he had wisdom. I didnt have to worry,he managed my house better than I did.

Host:

Then came the accusation

Potiphar:

My wife came to me with his robe in her hand. She said he tried to violate her. I was furious,embarrassed. I didnt know what to think.

Host (to Potiphars wife):

You saw Joseph every day. Why did you pursue him?

Potiphars Wife:

He was handsome. Confident. Different. I was married,but I was miserable. I wanted attention, and he had boundaries. That only made me want him more.

Host:

And when he refused you?

Potiphars Wife:

I felt small. Rejected. So I flipped the script. I screamed. I lied.

But the truth is,he ran. He didnt flirt. He didnt fold. He ran from me and into the next part of his story.

Host (to Joseph in audience):

You lost your robe,but you kept your righteousness.

Joseph:

Yes. Id rather lose the coat than lose my calling.

I may have been thrown into prison,but I walked in clean.

The Big Truth

Josephs refusal wasnt just about saying no to sin.

It was about saying yes to purpose,even if it meant temporary loss.

1. Favor Attracts Temptation

Genesis 39:6 Joseph was a goodly person, and well favored.

Sometimes what makes you stand out also makes you a target.

2. Every Opportunity Isnt Meant to Be Taken,Some Are Meant to Be Resisted

Joseph had the opportunity but he had standards.

Genesis 39:9 How then can I do this great wickedness, and sin against God?

3. False Accusation Doesnt Cancel Real Anointing

Joseph was lied on, locked up, and stripped of his robe,

But he still had his gift, his purpose, and Gods hand.

4. God Uses Injustice to Set Up Promotion

The prison wasnt punishment,it was preparation.

Joseph went down in Potiphars house so he could rise in Pharaohs.

Closing Prayer

Father,

Thank You for the example of Joseph.

For showing me that I dont have to compromise to be called.

Help me to run from what tempts me and stay faithful to what Youve placed in me.

Even if it costs me something,Id rather lose my robe than lose my righteousness.

And when the lies come, when the injustice hits

Remind me that You see, You know, and You will elevate in due time.

In Jesus name,

Amen.

Episode 52: Host & Jacob (Israel)

Theme: When a father speaks, generations shift.

Genesis 49:1 Gather yourselves together, that I may tell you that which shall befall you in the last days.

Opening Monologue

Tonights guest isnt here to wrestle with angels.

Hes not running from Esau or working for Laban.

Hes sitting,old, weathered, and wise,ready to release prophetic fire over the twelve sons who will become twelve tribes.

This isnt just a family gathering,

This is a generational transfer. A divine download.

He remembers their past but he also speaks into their future.

Please welcome the father of a nation

Jacob,also known as Israel,is back in the studio.

Interview: Host JacobIsrael

Host:

Israel. This is a fullcircle moment. Youve wrestled, wandered, and led. And now, youre sitting as a father over your sons. How does it feel?

343

Jacob:

Its humbling. Ive seen so much,betrayal, blessing, brokenness and now I get to speak into what will come after me.

Host:

You didnt just bless,you prophesied. Lets walk through some of these.

Quick Highlights of the Prophetic Blessings

Reuben The Firstborn:

Unstable as water, thou shalt not excel

You were my strength but your lack of control cost you position.

Simeon Levi The Hotheads:

Instruments of cruelty I will divide them

You fought for your sister,but with too much rage. That fire had no filter.

Judah The Leader:

The sceptre shall not depart from Judah

You made mistakes but you repented. And now kings will come through you.

344

Zebulun The Seafarer:

He shall dwell at the haven of the sea

A tribe that moves commerce and expansion.

Issachar The Wise Worker:

A strong donkey bearing burdens

Quiet strength. Service and discernment.

Dan The Judge:

Dan shall judge his people

A tribe of justice,though snakes may still slither in.

Gad The Warrior:

A troop shall overcome him: but he shall overcome at the last.

He may get hit,but he always gets up.

Asher The Provider:

Out of Asher his bread shall be fat

Blessing. Resource. Increase.

Naphtali The Free Spirit:

A hind let loose

Agility. Expression. A wordgiver.

Joseph The Fruitful One:

A fruitful bough whose branches run over the wall.

Rejected but preserved. Blessed beyond betrayal.

Benjamin The Fierce One:

Shall ravin as a wolf

Small but mighty. Loyal. Dangerous to his enemies.

Host:

You didnt hold back. Some words were hard,but honest.

JacobIsrael:

I spoke what God gave me. Some needed to be warned. Some needed to be reminded. And all needed to hear: You matter. Your tribe matters. The future needs your obedience.

Host:

What do you want this generation to know about speaking over their children?

JacobIsrael:

Bless them with honesty. Cover them with prayer.

Speak to their potential, not just their performance.

And let your last words be words that build futures.

346

The Big Truth

Jacobs final words werent just reflections,they were prophetic blueprints.

Your words can shape identity, direction, and destiny.

1. A Fathers Voice is a Bridge Between Generations

Jacob didnt just talk to sons,he spoke to tribes.

2. Truth is the Greatest Blessing You Can Give

He told the truth,whether it was blessing or rebuke.

Because real love doesnt flatter,it prepares.

3. The Blessing is Bigger Than the Person

What he spoke still echoes in history.

Because when Gods hand is on your words, they dont expire.

4. Your End Can Launch Someone Elses Beginning

As Jacob faded,Israel rose.

And a family became a nation.

347

Prayer

Father,

Thank You for every opportunity to speak life.

Let my words be filled with truth, love, wisdom, and legacy.

Teach me to bless boldly.

To correct with grace.

To speak into what my eyes cant yet see.

May my mouth carry heaven.

And may what I release build generations after me.

In Jesus name,

Amen.

End of Episode 52.

Final Word: Late Night Talk With the Word Season 1: Genesis

As the curtains close on Season 1 of Late Night Talk With the Word, we reflect on the incredible journey through the foundational book of Genesis. This season was more than just interviews and storytelling,it was a divine dive into the very beginning of it all. Genesis isnt just the first book of the Bible; its the book of beginnings, the blueprint of creation, the roots of humanity, and the unfolding of Gods original plan for redemption.

Weve had the honor of sitting down with some of the most iconic and complex figures in all of Scripture. From the voice of God speaking the world into existence, to the raw and vulnerable testimonies of Adam, Eve, and Cain, this season was filled with emotion, insight, correction, and comfort. We journeyed through the Garden, felt the weight of the first sin, watched the world drown in judgment and rise again through the obedience of Noah. We heard from Enoch, who walked so closely with God that he never saw death. We interviewed Sarah and Rebekah, who taught us the power of faith and waiting. We felt the heartbreak of Dinah, the boldness of Tamar, and the rise of Judah from mess to Messiahs line.

Josephs multiepisode arc took us from the pit to the palace, and in every conversation, we found a little more of ourselves in these stories. Whether we identified with the rejection, the delay, the mistakes, or the restoration, Genesis reminded us that God is present in every chapter of our lives.

Throughout this season, we laughed, cried, questioned,

350

and praised. Each interview brought the Bible to life in a new way, transforming pages into personal encounters. Characters who once seemed distant and ancient became relatable and real. And thats the power of Gods Word,it lives.

"For the word of God is quick, and powerful, and sharper than any twoedged sword and is a discerner of the thoughts and intents of the heart." , Hebrews 4:12 KJV

The book of Genesis shows us the depths of Gods creativity and the heights of His mercy. We saw His justice at work, but we also saw His grace never fail. From Eden to Egypt, Genesis is a story of a people chosen, a promise spoken, and a future already seen by God. Its the foundation upon which the rest of Scripture is built. Without Genesis, we wouldnt understand the significance of covenant, the weight of sin, or the glory of redemption.

"In the beginning God created the heaven and the earth." , Genesis 1:1 KJV

Every moment in Season 1 pointed back to that beginning,not just of time, but of truth. The truth that God created us with intention. That even when we fall, He doesnt abandon us. That His plans are bigger than our pasts. And that every broken thing in Genesis pointed forward to a Savior who would one day make all things new.

As we close the book on this season, we also want to remind every reader of the importance of staying in Gods Word. The Bible is not a textbook,its a lifeline. It is alive, breathing wisdom and instruction into every part of our daily journey.

351

It comforts in pain, convicts in weakness, corrects in error, and champions us in faith.

"Thy word is a lamp unto my feet, and a light unto my path." , Psalm 119:105 KJV

Reading the Word isnt just about gaining knowledge. Its about encountering God. And through the book of Genesis, we encountered Him as Creator, Judge, PromiseMaker, CovenantKeeper, and the ultimate Father who disciplines in love and provides in every season.

My prayer is that this book not only brought the stories of the Bible to life but brought you closer to the Author of them all. That as you read the interviews, monologues, big truths, and offer up a prayer, your heart was stirred to go back to the Word for yourself. Because nothing,no podcast, no book, not even Late Night Talk With the Word,can replace personal time in Scripture.

I pray that through this journey, you gained:

A deeper understanding of the people God used

A clearer picture of God's heart and holiness

A reminder that your story,like theirs,is still unfolding under Gods direction

Genesis isnt just history. Its your heritage. And the same God who walked with Adam, rescued Noah, renamed Jacob, and elevated Joseph,is still writing your story today.

So as we end Season 1 get ready.

Because Season 2 is coming.

And were headed to Exodus.

Chains will be broken. A nation will rise. Gods name will thunder through the wilderness. And deliverance will walk through fire and stand before Pharaoh.

Stay tuned for Late Night Talk With the Word: Season 2 Exodus.

See you in the next chapter.

Made in the USA
Middletown, DE
11 November 2025

21033821R00205